HOW DO I LOVE MY NEIGHBOR?

4 PROMISES AND 6 TRUTHS

JEFF FRICK

"In recent days, our nation has endured another round of civil unrest based on a myriad of issues such as, racism, biases, lack of cultural awareness, differences in political ideology, classism and several additional challenges that continue to plague us as a people. In times past the basic strategy in dealing with many of these challenges was to simply ignore them and hope they work themselves out. This book, "How Do I Love My Neighbor? (Four Promises and Six Truths)" authored by my dear brother, Chaplain Jeff Frick, plunges right into the heart of the matter and deals with the only solution, "Love." It is important for you to know, the words of this book are words written from the life experiences of Chaplain Jeff Frick, wonderful principles from the Word of God and the experiences of others. I know you will be blessed by this book and the strategies and principles in it. A special thanks to Chaplain Jeff for being obedient to the Will of God and sharing with us all the power and importance of sharing love with one another."

— **JAMES FRIEDMAN**, Senior Pastor/Managing Chaplain, Eastpointe, MI

"Jeff's love for Christ and his heart to see others know the love of God are on full display here. With each page, I pray you'll be inspired to 'love your neighbor' more, as I have been by my friendship with Jeff."

— J. ERIK BLEDSOE, President, Lifesong Ministries, Nashville, TN

"Our neighbor's welfare and our own are intimately connected. With great clarity and Biblical illustrations Chaplain Jeff Frick explains how to love your neighbor the way Jesus taught us. Forgive everybody 70 times 7 daily and speak Shalom to everyone."

— PASTOR BOB PYLE, Salem Brethren Church, Mt. Pleasant Mills, PA

"Jeff's first book is a pretty complete treatise on loving your 'neighbor.' He includes the aspects of love which we first think: being kind, gentle and serving but goes on to include and explain 'tough love.' For Jeff, this means caring enough to point out correction, trying to stop a friend from going down the wrong path or deeper in sin, or doesn't really want to change. I appreciate the sections on 'our words matter' and the importance of listening."

— JUDY DAGGETT, Former Newspaper Reporter/Editor, Rochester Hills, MI

"God chose Jeff to share his raw truths and life examples to gently guide you through this equation 'Grace + Truth + Time = Change.' Once we learn to stop self-serving, we are capable to begin loving our neighbor. Read it often until it becomes a natural way of living."

— CHAPLAIN MARIA DeKIMPE, Shelby Christian Fellowship Church, Shelby Twp., MI

"This book serves as a guided exploration of 'loving your neighbor.' The four promises and six truths are presented with humility and clarity. Clearly articulated personal examples effectively illustrate the use of promises and truths in daily life. This book will be a blessing to all who take the journey and to those who are 'truly loved' along the way."

— MELODIE KONDRATEK, Stephen Minister; Associate Professor, Rochester Hills, MI

"Jeff honors the authority of the Lord in his life, and he is a wise teacher and mentor to many. In his book, How Do I Love My Neighbor, he shares truths and relatable stories with us. Jeff's examples broadened my understanding and inspires me to be more intentional with whom God has entrusted around me. So many truths to walk away with like this one: we are vessels of God's love, instruments of God's peace, and reflectors of His light. Thank you for sharing the wisdom God gave you with us through your book."

— SONJA MALETTA, Campus Director Kensington Church, Clinton Twp., MI

"In my experience as a Pastor for the past 30 years, these 4 promises and 6 truths Jeff has laid out for us are invaluable for every Christian! This book is challenging, encouraging and insightful for anyone wanting to take their relationship with the Lord to the next level."

— CHRIS ZARBAUGH, Lead Teaching Pastor, Heritage Church, Sterling Hgts., MI

CONTENTS

MORE

© 2020 by GRAM Ministry

Published by:

Kingdom, Inc.
719 Lambs Creek Road
Mansfield, PA 16933
Kingdom.com

GRAM Ministry
48366 Whatley Court
Shelby Township, MI 48315
248.431.4051
Gramministry@gmail.com
Gramministry.org

Print ISBN: 978-1-883906-06-1

Cover design and interior formatting by *Hannah Linder Designs*
hannahlinderdesigns.com

Author: Jeff Frick

This book is dedicated to my beautiful son Michael.

Michael, you always gave the best hugs, and you were always ready to give a hug when someone needed it. Nothing can ever replace you my son. I learned so much about love from you. In your absence, you continue to teach me how to love. Not a day goes by that I don't think of you. I miss you so much Michael. I love you!
Dad

"We gon be alright, as long as we got two feet and a heartbeat" — Michael Frick

Thank you, Lord, for the wonderful gift of Michael

ACKNOWLEDGMENTS

I have many people to thank for helping me in the writing of this book.

I was inspired by a revelation from the Lord God to write this book. He spoke to me and said I was to use the information He gave me over my years of ministry. I went home and formulated the chapters and all the bullet points of information. Then I let life get in the way and set it aside for a while. I also drew inspiration from my son Michael, the way that he lived his life and how he loved people. Then, one day later that year, I was also encouraged by my very good friend Mike Lock. We were preparing for a ministry filming session and were discussing possible topics. I thought that we could use some of the material from this book, yet to be written. Mike abruptly said, "Absolutely not! This information is proprietary and needs to be copywritten before it is shared." Thank you, Mike, for your encouragement.

Many have helped with the most difficult process of editing this book and I would like to thank them. This list is pretty lengthy, but each of them deserves my gratitude for the countless hours in reading and re-reading this book. A special thank you goes out to Judy Daggett. She led the charge in the editing process. The names listed below made it possible for you, the reader, to receive the best achievable product.

Thank you, James Friedman!
Thank you, Loren Siffring!
Thank you, Chris Zarbaugh!
Thank you, Dave Green!
Thank you, Dave Torres!
Thank you, Chris Bokmuller!
Thank you, Judy Daggett!
Thank you, Maria DeKimpe!
Thank you, Ron Daggett!
Thank you, Nick Pruett!
Thank you, Andy Kelly!
Thank you, Mike Lock!
Thank you, Stephanie Adams, my sister!
And thank you, Laura Frick, my wife!

Because of all of you, this book is available to readers.

FOREWORD

If you would have told me even one year ago that I was going to write a book, I would have never believed you. I have seen God work miracles through my life in countless ways, but this book was definitely not something I saw coming. The day He told me to write it, I truly believed that I could complete it within a few weeks. I want to share with you that the book writing process is a lot of things, but it is certainly not easy nor is it quick. I found this experience to be exciting, fun, thought-provoking, therapeutic, healing, and a great test of patience. However, having now completed it I am extremely happy with what I have shared. This book represents many moments in my life both circumstantially and relationally. These moments were created by God and He told me to assemble them this way. To God be the glory!

I really do live by the 4 Promises and 6 Truths every day. If you ever encounter any of the men that I mentor and disciple, chances are they will find ways to direct your attention to these promises and truths when applicable. The 4 Promises and 6 Truths truly do bring a vivid and simplistic picture of what it means to love our neighbor. I hope to make certain that the 4 Promises and the 6 Truths are not meant to add to God's Word or to take the place of God's Word. They are the vehicle that helps me to apply God's Word and continue to grow in my understanding of what Jesus is saying to us about loving our neighbor in the Scriptures.

4 Promises:

1. I Will Never Judge You.
2. I Will Never Be Your "Yes" Man.
3. I Will Always Point You To Jesus.
4. I Will Always Have Open Arms Ready To Receive You.

6 Truths:

1. Once You Learn A New "Truth," You Cannot Unlearn It.
2. You Cannot Give Away What You Do Not Have.
3. You Cannot Make Someone Accept What They Are Unwilling To Receive.
4. You Cannot Take Someone To A Place You Have Never Been.
5. Time Is A Necessary Component For Understanding.
6. Grace + Truth + Time = Change.

I encourage you to not only read the book but to also apply the contents to your life. If you do, I promise you that God will demonstrate His marvelous magnificence in ways that you could never comprehend. The stories in this book are all real. I share them not as something I have read in a book, nor words I heard from a friend, nor a movie I watched, or even events I witnessed through others. I experienced every moment of every story, but they are just a glimpse of what He has done. Much of what I have shared centers around my service as a Chaplain. When you journey through my book, you will find many stories involving funerals, disease, and difficult life lessons.

I thank you for taking the time to read through what God has asked me to share with you. These promises and truths are a gift that God has given me as I have learned to love my neighbor over the years. Now I share them with you with a proven track record that they are effective and indeed work. By God's grace, I have seen much fruit in my ministry. I pray that He would bless you mightily.

"I continue to pray for your love to grow and increase beyond measure, bringing you into the rich revelation of spiritual insight in all things. This will enable you to choose the most excellent way of all—becoming pure and without offense until the unveiling of Christ. And you will be filled completely with the fruits of righteousness that are found in Jesus, the Anointed One—bringing great praise and glory to God"
(Philippians 1:9-11 TPT).

MAKE IT SIMPLE

There is a passage in the Gospel of Luke, Chapter 10, where Jesus is asked by an expert in the law, "What must I do to inherit eternal life?" Jesus demonstrates something extraordinary with His response. He asks two questions. "What is written in the Law? How do you read it?" Jesus asks the lawyer how he, a lawyer, interprets the Law. Jesus met the lawyer right where he was and asked questions the lawyer was certain to understand.

Instead of taking the conversation with this expert in the law to a different place, Jesus made it simple for the inquirer. Then, Jesus let the expert share his thoughts on the subject by listening. In doing so, Jesus both demonstrated and fulfilled the answer to the lawyer's question. The lawyer responded to Jesus' questions this way, "Love the Lord your God with all your heart and with all your soul and with all your strength and with all your mind and love your neighbor as yourself." After affirming the lawyer's response, Jesus stated, "If you do this, you will live."

Seems simple, right? The lawyer could not resist making this simple claim complicated. He had to ask another question, "Who is my neighbor?" Jesus responded with the parable about the 'Good Samaritan,' but why did the lawyer ask the final question? Many believe this question is rooted in the lawyer's desire, basic human nature, to love whom he chooses, not who God commands. However, this would not be the fulfillment of the law that he obviously claimed to understand. It was this incident in Scripture that took me on a journey to the enlightenment on how to love my neighbor.

THE PARABLE OF THE GOOD SAMARITAN

On one occasion an expert in the law stood up to test Jesus. "Teacher," he asked, "what must I do to inherit eternal life?" "What is written in the Law?" he replied. "How do you read it?" He answered, "'Love the Lord your God with all your heart and with all your soul and with all your strength and with all your mind'; and, 'Love your neighbor as yourself.'" "You have answered correctly," Jesus replied. "Do this and you will live." But he wanted to justify himself, so he asked Jesus, "And who is my neighbor?" In reply Jesus said: "A man was going down from Jerusalem to Jericho, when he was attacked by robbers. They stripped him of his clothes, beat him and went away, leaving him half dead. A priest happened to be going down the same road, and when he saw the man, he passed by on the other side. So too, a Levite, when he came to the place and saw him, passed by on the other side. But a Samaritan, as he traveled, came where the man was; and when he saw him, he took pity on him. He went to him and bandaged his wounds, pouring on oil and wine.

> *Then he put the man on his own donkey, brought him to an inn and took care of him. The next day he took out two denarii and gave them to the innkeeper. 'Look after him,' he said, 'and when I return, I will reimburse you for any extra expense you may have.' "Which of these three do you think was a neighbor to the man who fell into the hands of robbers?" The expert in the law replied, "The one who had mercy on him." Jesus told him, "Go and do likewise." (Luke 10:25-37)*

My friend and mentor, Dr. Loren Siffring, told me that man complicates everything and therefore creates obstacles for himself. He said to me more times than I can count, *"make everything simple."* When things are simple, they are easily understood, transferable, and create the greatest impact.

I internalized those words and began to examine what that might look like in my own life especially as it relates to the idea of loving my neighbor. As a result, many questions began to flood my mind. After much contemplation, the seeking of wisdom, prayer, and application I believe God spoke to me. The result is a lifelong desire to know Him and then to give away what He continues to lavish on us. The content of this book is what I have found to be distinctively evident in my own experience of trying to hear from God and walk in obedience. This book is my *simple* understanding of how to love my neighbor.

I began to formalize my thoughts and ideas of what this command of God to "love my neighbor" was truly saying and at the same time I desperately wanted to hear what Jesus was saying directly to me about it. I began to write my thoughts on paper. After assembling all that I thought this command meant, I started the process of simplifying all my thoughts into the shallowest of pools and yet deepest of oceans. How could I make this make sense to me, and to anyone else who may read it and at the same time capture the depth of my human thoughts and begin to move closer to what God is leading us to do in these words?

What came to me is what I call the 4 Promises and 6 Truths. I have been living these out in all my relationships for many years now. I hope to make certain that the 4 Promises and 6 Truths are not meant to add to God's Word or to take the place of God's Word. They are the vehicle that helps me to apply God's Word and continue to grow in my under-standing of what Jesus is saying to us about loving our neighbor in the Scriptures.

WHAT DO PEOPLE SEE?

After I incorporated the 4 Promises and 6 Truths as a part of my everyday practice, I could see strong evidence that there was value in this, and that God was in the midst of it all. One of the many blessings in my life is the "calling" that God placed on me to disciple (mentor) men. I began to ask myself if the practice of loving my neighbor through the command of God and by sharing the 4 Promises and 6 Truths was evident in the way men would continue to return week after week, month after month, and year after year. It became abundantly clear that there was, and is, rich significance in this. God began to illuminate certain Scriptures for me. I remember the first time this happened. I was reading *Daniel 5:11* when God spoke to me, *"There is a man in your kingdom who has the spirit of the holy gods in him. In the time of your father he was found to have insight and intelligence and wisdom like that of the gods. Your father, King Nebuchadnezzar, appointed him chief of the magicians, enchanters, astrologers and diviners."*

This part of the Book of Daniel is titled "The Writing on the Wall." What is happening in this moment of the story is that King Nebuchadnezzar has died and his grandson, King Belshazzar, has taken over as king and is having a great banquet. The only problem is King Belshazzar decides to use the gold goblets that were taken from the temple of God in Jerusalem when his grandfather besieged the city many years earlier. Along with the articles of gold, Daniel was one of the many young men brought to Babylonia against their will for the king's service. Drinking from the goblets, the king and his guests began praising the gods of gold and silver, bronze and iron, wood and stone. Suddenly, the fingers of a human hand appeared to write on the wall and the king was so frightened that he turned pale. This is when verse 11 comes into play as the queen reminds everyone of Daniel. Daniel was now somewhere around 80 years old and had lived in Babylonia for many years. Nobody actually cared about Daniel until they were in trouble and needed him. And now, that was the case. How did the people know to ask for Daniel? The reason is that Daniel presented himself the same way every day. He was described as having the spirit of the holy gods in him. Daniel walked with the Lord and his faith was not bound in circumstances but solely rooted in God.

After God spot-lighted this verse, a question kept ringing in my spirit, "What do people see when you walk into the room?" This is a question I ask every man that I disciple. Why is this important? Remember, Daniel presented himself the same to everyone, his integrity and consistency were never in question no matter the situation. So, you can be the quiet guy, the funny guy, the sports guy, the talkative guy, the political guy, any guy you want to be, or you can be the guy who walks with the Lord. Why is this important? People will absorb you to the depth of their boundaries. These limits are based on both the frequency and the duration of your meetings. Why is that important? If you are the person walking with the Lord, most everyone will eventually come to respect you because you never waver in your beliefs, always presenting yourself the same. Our attempt to reach the lost is not found in a great message, it's found in the integrity of our consistent demonstration of beliefs.

Let me repeat, if we honor the authority of the Lord in our own lives, others will respect the Lord's authority in us! Not everyone will want to hear about the Lord from you, but they will take comfort that you are a resource they can come to when they have a need. When they are in trouble, they are lost, or their life is in turmoil, you will be the one they call. It is in their moments of despair they will come to realize you have always loved them as your neighbor and never pushed them beyond their boundaries. You simply met them right where they are.

OUR MELODY WITHIN

Sometime later, God further bolstered this thought through another verse in Scripture. This time He spoke to me by illuminating this verse, *"We saw him with our very own eyes. We gazed upon him and heard him speak. Our hands actually touched him, the one who was from the beginning, the Living Expression of God," (1 John 1:1 TPT).* What came alive in this verse is that it says our hands actually touched Him. When I dug deeper into the meaning of this, I found something rather unique. The word touch is poetic. It comes from a sensory verb meaning "to pluck the strings of an instrument." It is as though John is saying, "We have plucked the chords of Jesus' being and felt what motivated Him, His melody within." What do people see when you walk into a room? How long would it take before someone would pluck the chords within you and know who you are, what you believe, and the melody that lies within you? In loving our neighbor, this is an element that matters.

Consistency is closely related to the question raised previously, "What do people see when you walk into the room." We have all heard of or known a person who is brand new in their faith and he or she is running around sharing this new faith with everyone, but mostly they are scaring everyone around them. Their intensity is exuberant, but it draws very few people to faith because it looks very little like love. One's intensity should never overshadow their consistency. Learning how to love someone is learning what the other person's needs are and meeting that person right where they are. If we truly love them, we are not controlling the pace, we simply walk with them. We are not in front of them, dragging them, nor are we behind them, pushing.

Remember, if our intensity is overshadowing our consistency, we are not loving our neighbor. And, let me state very clearly that consistency is also strongly attached to punctuality and integrity. If you say you will meet someone or call someone at a certain time, be ready to demonstrate consistency. This will show the other person that you value them and in this, they will experience your love.

NOT MY WILL, BUT YOURS BE DONE

Obedience is probably the single most difficult thing for us to present to God. Every day we are all in a battle of the flesh and the power of the wills. Will we surrender to God's Will or will our will be done? God's command to love our neighbor cannot be done on our terms, we must be willing to walk in obedience. We must surrender our desire to be in charge of the outcome, even if we are certain of what needs to take place. Too many of us believe we know what's best especially when it comes to our own lives. We proudly call ourselves good because we believe our hearts are pure. When we attempt to control the outcome or we are anxious to see the fruit of our labor or we try to create our specific results, we have made whatever task we are doing all about us. When it's all about us, it is never about God. If it's not about God, we are not loving our neighbor.

Pretend there are 10 homeless people in your path today. What would you do? Most people would say that they feel the need to help each of the homeless people. Maybe they buy each person a meal, maybe they give money, maybe they just sit and have a conversation with them. None of these outcomes sound bad at first glance. In fact, they seem like the right thing to do. But what did God say? Did we ask Him? What if God said, "Yes, help all of them." What if God said, "Only help five of them." What if God said, "Help only one of them." And what if God said, "Walk past all of them." I know what you're thinking. Why would God ask me to walk past all of these homeless people and not help them? To tell you the truth, I have no idea if God would say that or not.

My point is that if we never ask God what we should do, we are *not* obedient. We'll never know or even realize that God asked us to walk past 10 homeless people because on the other side of the street there is a single mother with three young children and her circumstances are dire. She is almost to the point of becoming homeless herself. Because you asked God what He wanted you to do instead of attempting to control outcomes, this young family might have their lives changed forever. God often prompts us to give our time, energy, and resources to help those He places in our path. Not necessarily the ones we see through our eyes. Obedience to God and not looking to create our outcomes is more important than we can ever imagine. *"Blessed are all who fear the Lord, who walk in obedience to him" (Psalm 128:1).*

WITH GOD, THERE'S ALWAYS MORE

Some of you reading this book will understand exactly what I am about to say. If we can attain some measure of consistency and obedience while presenting ourselves the same in every circumstance, when we walk into a room people will see a person who does not waver. Many will seek us out. I know that some of you have already experienced this. It's sort of like becoming flypaper to flies, a magnet to steel, or honey to bears. What I am eluding to is that many people will seek to grab your attention to ask you questions because they believe you will provide greater insight than they may currently possess. If you have already experienced this in your own life, you know exactly what I mean. Sometimes this can be daunting because it is time-consuming, but there is no mistaking that this is another aspect of loving your neighbor.

When you are willing to listen intently to other people and provide them space to share their concerns, you are demonstrating the love that God has lavished on you. In a world where we are all rushing to get to the next important event on our ever-expanding calendar, just a few uninterrupted moments with a person can provide the greatest testament of God's love. By doing this, we will love our neighbor and leave people better than we found them.

Learning to love our neighbor is a process of receiving from God all that He has for us. We can learn to hear His voice, learn to die-to-self and surrender to His will continuously, forever. One of the most *joyous* aspects of God is that there is always more. Just as our faith can grow to greater depths, our ability to love our neighbor can always expand as well.

To provide an example for all that Chapter 1 contains, I will share a story from my life. I have had the pleasure of sitting under my mentor, Loren, for many years. Loren approached me one day and asked if I would like to be ordained by him. We had the appropriate conversations, prayed, and decided to set a date for the event. While waiting for the date to come, many of the men I disciple were informed by me that this ordination was planned, and they were encouraged to attend.

One day while sitting with Dave, a man that I disciple, he decided to comment on the ordainment. "Gosh Jeff, you must have been working at this for a very long time." After a brief reflection, I responded to Dave in this way, "No, and yes!" Dave said he was confused by my answer. So, I clarified, "Dave, the ordainment was never my focus. This wonderful opportunity was never on my radar nor was it my goal. All I did was walk with the Lord because He asked me to. I did not expect ever being bestowed an honor such as ordainment. However, because I was obedient, consistent, and did not attempt to create any outcomes thereby leaving God in charge, this opportunity was a blessing that God could shower on me. With God, there's always more."

God will bless us beyond what we can ever imagine if we

just learn to be His instrument. *"My flesh and my heart may fail, but God is the strength of my heart and my portion forever" (Psalm 73:26).*

A GARDEN HOSE

The remaining chapters of this book outline the 4 Promises and 6 Truths in more detail. Each chapter is dedicated to a single surety. I hope that you find as much value in digesting them as I have. The 4 Promises and 6 Truths have served me well over the years and have helped me learn to love my neighbor in a more far-reaching way. Everything we receive from God we are called to share with others generously. *"Remember this: Whoever sows sparingly will also reap sparingly, and whoever sows generously will also reap generously" (2 Corinthians 9:6).* Pouring out all that we have like a drink offering is to think of ourselves as a garden hose. *"But even if I am being poured out like a drink offering on the sacrifice and service coming from your faith, I am glad and rejoice with all of you" (Philippians 2:17).* Like a garden hose, we have two jobs. First, distribute the water (information). Second, don't kink! Whoever God chooses to proclaim these truths is not as important as that they are delivered. What's the best thing about being a *garden hose for God*? The hose gets the first drink, the cool life-giving water from God flowing through the hose and then into others.

<u>4 Promises:</u>

1- I Will Never Judge You.

2- I Will Never Be Your "Yes" Man.

3- I Will Always Point You To Jesus.

4- I Will Always Have Open Arms Ready To Receive You.

<u>6 Truths:</u>

1- Once You Learn A New "Truth," You Cannot Unlearn It.

2- You Cannot Give Away What You Do Not Have.

3- You Cannot Make Someone Accept What They Are Unwilling To Receive.

4- You Cannot Take Someone To A Place You Have Never Been.

5- Time Is A Necessary Component For Understanding.

6- Grace + Truth + Time = Change.

Could the 4 Promises and 6 Truths become chords within each of us, that others would pluck, thus discovering our motivation, our melody within?

2

PROMISE #1

I WILL NEVER JUDGE YOU

O ne of the most wonderful things you can give to any person is acceptance. Each of us has this built-in desire to be accepted, to be valued, and to be loved. We come to find out over time that only God can truly fill these needs. However, when people start with the great intention of loving their neighbor, acceptance can happen and be overwhelmingly beautiful.

Promise #1 is *"I Will Never Judge You."* I have found that this lead promise is the greatest gift you can offer someone. Some people are intuitively able to share elements of their life spontaneously while others require many encounters with the same person to feel safe enough to open up at all. Either person will only share what they know will not leave them vulnerable or fearful of being judged. Setting the table with this opening arrangement is something many people find strange but at the same time refreshing. Also, let me make sure to add that confidentiality should always be tightly entwined in this non-judgmental atmosphere. The people I have the privilege of spending time with know with certainty they are in a safe place.

In my years of ministry, I have witnessed many beautiful moments where both men and women have exposed their feelings and made themselves vulnerable and open. These occurrences always amaze me because only God could create such beautiful tender moments. In fact, they happen so often, I have come to expect to be astounded. Why are so many people finding acceptance elusive, even from family and close friends? The simple answer is our culture is far from God. In a later chapter of this book, we will talk in detail about the concept of "You cannot give away what you do not have."

An entire book could be written on what happens when we become autonomous, removing God from our life. We must not forget that God designed us to live in community and to walk in obedience. Sadly, many have never fully submitted to His authority. The world is too enticing for many of us. We are blinded and thus convince ourselves that we are good, our motives are pure, and we can be the author of love. When we become the author of love, we end up giving away a cheap version of love, something known as *favor*. Favor is something we have to earn; therefore, it is void of love. ***"Dear friends, let us love one another, for love comes from God. Everyone who loves has been born of God and knows God. Whoever does not love does not know God, because God is love" (1 John 4:7-8).*** Never judging a person is the willingness to love that person simply for who they are, not for what they can do, not for what they can offer, not even for who we hope they become. When we love others, there can be no discrepancy. As Christians, our words and actions must always be in alignment.

It has been said that we have no virtue if we refuse to love the unlovable.

FATHER, I THANK YOU THAT NO PEOPLE GROUP IS

EXCLUDED FROM YOUR GREAT LOVE. TEACH US TO
TRULY LOVE ONE ANOTHER, AS YOU HAVE
GENEROUSLY LOVED US. HELP US TO LIVE OUT YOUR
COMMAND TO LOVE OUR NEIGHBOR.

GOD IS THE TRACTOR, WE ARE
THE PLOW

Before we graduate to a righteous person who will never pass judgment, we may have to experience moments where we thought we had everything under control but failed anyway. Moments, where our hearts burn with jealousy, pride, arrogance, and anger, can be a good thing. Yes, we probably kept these thoughts from escaping our lips, but God knows they live in our hearts. These unsuccessful moments can bring great clarity and growth if we let them. I have found these kinds of moments draw me closer to the One who can bring the necessary changes in our life. *"For the word of God is quick, and powerful, and sharper than any twoedged sword, piercing even to the dividing asunder of soul and spirit, and of the joints and marrow, and is a discerner of the thoughts and intents of the heart" (Hebrews 4:12 KJV).*

I was attending a weekend retreat. This retreat assembled men for three days at designated tables designed to build intimate relationships. We gathered with the other seven tables corporately for worship and the breaking of bread. Each table had a leader and a sub-leader, our table leader was Bill. Bill appeared to me as uneducated and not the best communicator. He had an awkwardness that I did not appreciate when I arrived. For the first two days, all I could think about was how and why this seemingly irrelevant man could be our table leader. I spent more than 48 hours comparing myself with Bill. Surely, I could do a better job than he! Surely, I was more mature in my faith than he! Surely, I would gain little to no understanding of God, Jesus, or the Holy Spirit while Bill was at the helm! All these thoughts, and more, flooded my mind.

Over the weekend, we heard 15 teachings, some from pastors, some from the organizers of the retreat, and some from table leaders. The teachings and who conveyed them were never announced beforehand. On the last day, Sunday, my table leader Bill delivered one of the teachings. At first, I was surprised. How could this organization allow this man who lacks the eloquence of speech to be in this position? Bill began to talk. As one might predict, his words were difficult to understand, and he labored to get comfortable. But something amazing happened very shortly after the teaching began. Bill began to share his testimony and his speech cleared and boldness set in.

We all heard an astonishing story of how God assaulted a man's life with a miracle upon miracle. You could have heard a pin drop. As Bill shared each glorious moment, my pride and ego began to depart. In their place was a constant stream of tears. Bill, a dairy farmer, belabored through long, hard days that would make most men quit. He worked a full-time job off-site, took care of the cows, and still managed to find time to be a dad and a husband. At night, when he was supposed to be sleeping, Bill would open God's Word and the Holy Spirit taught him how to read. Bill was especially gifted with the ability to communicate with intellectually and developmentally disabled children. He shared some of his most joyous moments where only God could have produced such outcomes. The last thing I remember Bill sharing was that he had become the Sunday School Teacher at his church. God had taught Bill to read, and it was his profound joy to share with the children at his church.

Bill's talk ended, but for nearly four hours afterward, my tears would not stop falling. God did a work in me that day. I looked right through a man and thought he was insignificant. I passed judgment on him. All the things I thought were true about Bill, were actually true about me. Bill was honest, humble, meek, righteous, holy, and God-fearing. I will never forget Bill. I praise God every day for providing the privilege of sitting with Bill and hearing his talk. A simple man with a simple message, "God is the tractor, we are the plow!" I thought I knew God, but Bill opened a window I had never gazed through before. Thank you, Jesus!

MEMORIAL OF ACCEPTANCE

A few years ago, I was asked to facilitate a funeral where I witnessed two groups of people mourning the same person but from different vantage points. One group had obviously felt acceptance from the deceased while the other group had not. When the day was over, I reflected on what God allowed me to observe and began to pray to ask what He wanted me to know. God is always drawing us closer to Him by revealing His character. The question is, are we willing to see and hear His prompts? Still, it was not until the drive home from the funeral service that God illuminated this event in my mind with great clarity.

The image God clarified started to unfold before the funeral as I sat with the adult children of the deceased man to learn who their father was and how he lived his life. The siblings informed me that their parents divorced many years ago and they had had little to do with their father. They shared that he was a business owner and had employed many people. The type of people he preferred to employ were those who may not be able to find employment elsewhere because of questionable backgrounds. Beyond these few details, there was not much else for me to speak about in the service concerning this man. I was beginning to see evidence the children had not found acceptance from their father.

When I arrived at the funeral home the next day, there were many more people than I had envisioned being in attendance based on what information I had been given. I greeted the siblings upon entering and was then introduced to an additional brother. At that time, I asked the family if anyone was planning on standing up to share during the service. They all said "no" they would not and added that they did not want anyone else to share either.

At most funerals, when the service is complete, the funeral director will greet the crowd and inform them of the family's requests before exiting. At this funeral, that did not happen. Upon completion of my service, I waited in the parlor, as usual, to make certain that all of the family's needs had been met. Unexpectedly, men started to walk up to the podium and speak of the deceased. After four or five men spoke, I realized that they were the dead man's employees. Still, my job was to meet the family's needs and I felt like that was not happening as their request for no other persons to speak was tossed aside. Just then, the last man stood at the podium. He was dressed in dirty work attire and his appearance was intimidating. This man was large, very muscular, and had many tattoos, not someone you would want to meet alone in a dark alley if appearances meant anything. Then this very large man began to cry uncontrollably. After collecting himself, he said only one thing, "No man ever told me he loved me, but this man did!" *"And now these three remain: faith, hope and love. But the greatest of these is love" (1 Corinthians 13:13).*

Suddenly, the image God was sharing became sharper. I began to thank God for allowing me to witness such a marvelous moment of raw emotion, as it is not very common for men to openly share their feelings. On the drive home, God clarified the events for me. How could the children of the deceased man not find acceptance from their father, and at the same time the employees could be swimming in it? The depth of the power of acceptance through the lens of loving our neighbor is beyond compare. One group of people hiding, not wanting anyone to know that they had not felt accepted, and the other willing to break cultural barriers because they had experienced something so grand. Both were mourning the same person.

THE 'MIME' EXPERIENCE

Coincidentally, in the closing moments of every funeral service that I perform I share what I refer to as "Insights for better relationships." One of those insights reads this way; "never let your kindness be so foreign that people are surprised." In *Galatians 5:22-23,* we read, *"But the fruit of the Spirit is love, joy, peace, forbearance, kindness, goodness, faithfulness, gentleness and self-control. Against such things there is no law."* The interesting thing about kindness is that it is neatly nestled right in the middle of the fruit of the Spirit. Scripture also reminds us that we are to clothe ourselves with righteousness. *"Therefore, as God's chosen people, holy and dearly loved, clothe yourselves with compassion, kindness, humility, gentleness and patience" (Colossians 3:12).* Without these characteristics, one can never truly offer Promise #1, *"I Will Never Judge You"* to anyone. For it is only because of God's kindness and patience He prevents His judgment for those who think they are beyond judgment. By His power, those walking in the Spirit can exhibit these character traits. For unbelievers, those not walking in the Spirit, no one among you can manifest these characteristics. So, apart from God, we are not able to fulfill Promise #1, *"I Will Never Judge You."*

In keeping on the theme of kindness, I would like to share what I have witnessed through many of my interactions. Most people, but especially men, are challenged to find a venue where the word kindness would ever leave a person's lips. It's not a popular word in our culture so we don't often hear it. At the same time, if we rarely speak it, how would we easily identify it? Thinking again about the fruit of the Spirit, the first three are God's gifts to us (love, joy, peace), the second three are how we treat others through our interactions (forbearance, kindness, goodness), the remaining three are how we demonstrate the transformative changes within us (faithfulness, gentleness, self-control).

Notice once again that kindness requires interaction. Earlier I shared with you one of my insights for better relationships, "Never let your kindness be so foreign that people are surprised." What I usually witness in other men because kindness is so rare, is what I like to describe as the "mime" experience. Remember, most people are truly surprised by kindness. In fact, I would go as far as to say that they seem to stand at a distance, almost like an invisible forcefield is holding them out. At the same time, they are fearful to enter because they are not willing to trust that this kindness is authentic. They are met with a decision to allow themselves to be vulnerable and experience the kindness offered to them or stand at a distance in disbelief. I cannot even begin to count the number of occasions where I have witnessed this seesaw battle take place within a man. I do recall *one* instance where a man allowed himself to become vulnerable and experience kindness rather quickly instead of holding his hands up like a "mime."

PRAYER FOR A PRISON INMATE

One Sunday at church, I was approached by a young adult man who I had never met. He asked if I would pray for him. I said I would, and then asked him what he wanted to pray about? I received no reply, he just bowed his head. I proceeded to pray for him, and he went on his way. A month later he returned. He asked again, "Would you pray for me? I really need some prayer." This time his demeanor was different, so I asked him if he would like to pray in a private prayer room? Now sitting at the table, in the prayer room, he disclosed what he wanted and why he needed prayer. As it turned out this young man was headed to prison. Austin was to turn himself in the day before Thanksgiving. This left him only three and a half weeks of freedom. We prayed together and then shared some small talk. Knowing Austin had just a short time remaining, I asked him if he would like to join me for the next three weeks at our Tuesday night men's Bible study group? He indicated that he did not have a vehicle, so I offered to pick him up and drive him. To my surprise, Austin agreed.

In the first two weeks, he and I were the only ones who

knew what awaited him. It was not until the end of the night on the second week, as we were praying corporately, that Austin disclosed his circumstances to the group. The men were astounded! This young man was so joyous, they were in disbelief. They thought, how could someone so young with such a heavy burden on his shoulders be so full of peace and joy? Austin was equally astonished that he was welcomed as one of the men. Even after disclosing his fate, he felt no shame from the men, only acceptance.

In the week before he was to turn himself in, the men's group pooled their money and purchased Austin a Bible. On that final night, each man, over 100 in total, signed the Bible. At the end of the night, the Bible was presented to Austin. After he shared his thankfulness, the entire men's group laid hands on Austin and prayed over him, anointed his head with oil, and hugged him. It was such a special moment. God certainly showed up that night.

On the ride back to his parent's house, Austin was very quiet. He was reading the names of all the signatures in his new Bible. I could tell that he was reeling from what he had just experienced. I have to admit that I too was overwhelmed. WOW! I thought, "God, You never cease to amaze me!" When we pulled up in the driveway, I was ill-prepared for what was to happen next. I thank God every day for allowing me to experience these types of moments, but when they occur so rapidly, it's hard to take them all in. Austin began to lose control of his body and then his words. He began to cry so profusely I thought he might need oxygen. Time was not important, as we were both *in* the moment, this wonderful, gracious, joyous, fantastic moment.

Austin, now only sobbing, began to regain the ability to utter words. He made only two statements. "I did not know that men lived this way. I don't know how to thank you." I reminded Austin that I only offered an invitation, nothing more. I pointed out he could have said "no." God wasn't finished yet. At that moment, I heard God clearly say to me, "Walk with him." I told Austin that I would make the arrangements and come to visit him in prison. He was delighted.

The rest of Austin's story would require many more chapters, but it concludes with an intimate concert of prayer and worship in his parent's living room some two-plus years later, the day after his release, one day after Christmas. My friend Dave and I made the trip every 6-8 weeks to the penitentiary that housed Austin during his prison term.

When you walk in obedience, God might take you on a completely unexpected journey, one where you would show boundless commitment to the least of these. I want to be very clear, Promise #1, *"I Will Never Judge You"* requires acceptance, kindness, and love. All of which are impossible apart from God. ***"Jesus looked at them and said, 'With man this is impossible, but not with God; all things are possible with God'" (Mark 10:27).***

3

PROMISE #2

I WILL NEVER BE YOUR "YES" MAN

When was the last time you examined the landscape of your environment and realized that the bulk of your friends have the same values as you do? Like draws like. People naturally mix with those who are similar and communicate with those of matching interests. In fact, we find it extremely difficult to even tolerate people who have very differing thoughts or opinions. So, to avoid difficult conversations or the possibility of conflict, we tend to match up with very parallel thinking and believing people. In doing so we form groups, sometimes referred to as tribes, which help us protect our beliefs.

Apart from the division these groups inherently cause, there are actually two more disparaging problems that emerge. First, these groups are stunted in terms of learning and growing because no one is challenging them to think or behave differently. Divisions tend to grow wider as each group becomes more cemented in their philosophy. Second, we slander and cut people with our words, those who may think and act differently than our tribe. We do this for self-protection. A Hebrew word describes this. *"But I tell you that anyone who is angry with a brother or sister will be subject to judgment. Again, anyone who says to a brother or sister, 'Raca,' is answerable to the court. And anyone who says, 'You fool!' will be in danger of the fire of hell"* (Matthew 5:22).

When you *Raca'* someone, you render them less than; you are on your way to murdering them with your heart and mind. If we spend our days living in division, because of beliefs and behaviors, and at the same time we surround ourselves with people of like mind, how do we begin to challenge those around us? How can we promise to never be a "yes" man?

In thinking about Promise #2, *"I Will Never Be Your 'Yes' Man,"* we must begin at the root. Every choice we make is followed by a consequence. There is an interesting thing to know about our consequences; they either benefit a person or they are a detriment to a person. Consequences never leave you the same, as they are never neutral. Sometimes consequences make their face known in the moment of decision, and sometimes consequences don't appear for days, weeks, months, or even years. If you desire to love your neighbor and you know that choices bring consequences, it becomes easier to point out a bad choice instead of going with the flow.

Thus, loving your neighbor and not becoming someone's "yes" man, is helping people construct favorable consequences by making good choices. You become the person who communicates to others not what they *want* to hear but what they *need* to hear. In other words, you are a true friend, not a "yes" man. This is how God calls us to love our neighbor.

BUILD UP OR TEAR DOWN?

"The words of the reckless pierce like swords, but the tongue of the wise brings healing" (Proverbs 12:18). We should be very concerned about the words we speak to others. To be known as the person who will share difficult truth, requires maturity, integrity, humility, courage, and love. Our words have incredible power. Remember, every word and/or action either builds a person up or tears a person down. Still, that does not mean that every person wants to hear the Truth. In fact, some people may avoid you because they fear they will be subject to the Truth. This makes what we say and how we speak vastly important. Do our words hurt or heal, confuse, or enlighten? Do our words whisper trust or communicate fear?

What we hope to make crystal clear to every person is that we are not here to judge, only to show that we love and care for them. If people know that we are 'for' them and 'not against' them, they are more likely to receive our words. If you saw a person that was about to be run over by a truck, would you not scream, "Get out of the way?" The answer, of course, is *yes* you step in because certain death awaits in this example. I have often asked that question to the people that I encounter in an attempt to further illustrate my point. Should we not treat every personal encounter in the same manner? If every course word, bad choice, or dubious behavior has the potential to bring death to our relationships, why would we treat any circumstance or choice differently than another? At a minimum, would we at least pose the question, "are you sure?" Ponder your motives before you speak or act, but love people enough to never be their "yes" man! Let us live in such a way that we never need to be remorseful due to our poor choice of words. *"Those who guard their mouths and their tongues keep themselves from calamity" (Proverbs 21:23).*

COMPANION OF FOOLS

"Walk with the wise and become wise, for a companion of fools suffers harm" (Proverbs 13:20). We are the average of the five people we hang out with the most. We are products of our environment. The values, morals, principles, and behaviors we display are the result of these close relationships taking root in us over time. This is why Scripture reminds us to choose our friends carefully. I remember sitting with a young married couple a few years back. Their marriage was in trouble for various reasons, but the most pressing problem was the result of infidelity. They both claimed to want to restore their relationship, but the wife was the one attempting to offer grace. The husband was the one who violated the sacred trust of the covenant.

One night on their way to my office, the wife texted me and shared that emotions might run high when they arrive because the husband had cheated once again with the same person. When I began to ask the husband what had taken place, I reminded him that he and his wife approached me to help them learn to restore their marriage. If his desire had changed, there was no need for us to continue to meet. The husband stated that he wanted to make his marriage work and began to explain what had happened. He shared that he had introduced his mistress to a group of his friends while they all hung out at a weekend get-away.

In response to this information, I asked these questions, "Which one of the many people that you mentioned pulled you aside and asked who is this woman?" "Which one of these people asked about your wife?" "Which one of these people reminded you about your children?" "How many of them warned you about the negative effects of divorce and blended family?" His reply to me was stunning. The husband informed me that not a single person asked him any of those types of questions. I responded this way, "Sir, does this not scare you? If I had paraded a strange woman in front of my circle of friends and not one person asked a probing question, that would scare me to death. I thought you said these people were your friends? Friends care about us, they want what's best for us, they want what's best for our family. These people do not sound like friends to me."

The husband knew he had no answer that could rebut anything I had asked, so he remained silent. I ended our conversation that night with this statement, "Sir, I will never be your 'yes' man. You came here for help and that is what I will provide. I know your marriage has many problems, but I can assure you that whatever has taken place, whatever your wife may have done, she did not deserve you cheating on her and leaving your family in this place of uncertainty. You have to decide right now if you are in this for the long haul." He agreed. We don't always make good choices, none of us are free to boast about perfect virtue, but do we surround ourselves with those who we trust can help us reduce the possibility of making poor choices?

PREPARATION FOR WHAT IS
TO COME

"Let your conversation be always full of grace, seasoned with salt, so that you may know how to answer everyone" (Colossians 4:6). Sometimes our experiences prepare us for what may come in the future. As my mentor always says, "Everything is preparation for what is to come." Having spent all but the first nine years of my life in a single-parent home or a blended family, God has gifted me with the ability to speak to men who are facing divorce. As many of you know, this can be one of the most painful experiences a person can endure. Even when circumstances have yet to unfold, Promise #2, *"I Will Never Be Your 'Yes' Man"* is fundamental. I recall when a friend of mine, Mike, was in this very season of life. Mike was attempting to hold his marriage together because he did not see the divorce coming and certainly did not want his marriage to end. He did inform me sometime later, after some reflection, that he could now see the warning signs but in the midst of it all he was blinded.

As you can imagine, Mike was very angry about the whole situation. Early in our conversations, I reminded Mike that he was entitled to be angry. I also reminded him he was not entitled to hurt other people because of his anger. I would not let him justify his position because there was more to think about than himself. I challenged Mike to never speak a coarse word about his soon to be ex-wife. If he allowed the anger in his heart to spill out through his words, his children would be sure to hear them. I reinforced to Mike that someone had to be the "constant" that his children would need during this tumultuous time. I appealed to Mike, to be that person.

There were many times during his divorce proceedings that Mike would ask me to review a text or email that he planned to send to his almost ex-wife. Most of those messages never made it to their destination. Part of helping someone do the right thing is never being their "yes" man. Although this process was sure to stretch Mike to his limits, it also helped him grow to become the person he is today. If you ask Mike about it, he would be sure to tell you that it was not pleasant, especially in those moments, but he would not trade the experience for anything.

Who are those you have surrounded yourself with? Do they want what's best for you? Do they love you enough to not let you justify your position? Will they never be your "yes" man?

WHAT – WHEN - HOW

"Instead, speaking the truth in love, we will grow to become in every respect the mature body of him who is the head, that is, Christ" (Ephesians 4:15). As I stated earlier, knowing what to say when to say it, and how to say it is crucial to not inadvertently *Raca'* people in the process. The road to hell is paved with good intentions, or so they say. This fact cannot be understated. Learning to use our words to lift, encourage, and challenge instead of tearing people down is not easy. Walking with God and growing in our faith certainly can help us along this footpath more expediently. Relying on God, receiving His grace, peace, and love is essential. Because the truth of it all is that none of us can become this reflection of Jesus without walking with Him daily. If there is no evidence of integrity and faith in your life, no person will ever receive your words in kindness. Your words will never feel inviting apart from the Power of the Holy Spirit, and if there is no measure of God's character in you, people will reject your words like they are judgment and self-righteousness.

Remember, we are to emulate our Lord and Savior, Christ

Jesus, in all that we do and share His love, in the same way, He has showered His love upon us.

SPEAKING OBSCENITIES

"Out of the same mouth come praise and cursing. My brothers and sisters, this should not be" (James 3:10). There came a time when I found myself sitting among a group of Christian men who were talking about how to confront people, whether Christian or not, about cursing and taking the Lord's name in vain. These conversations are always interesting because many people are fearful to interact in these matters. As we went around the room, hearing from those who decided they were brave enough to share, it surprised me that not one Christian man thought that he could do it. Some of the men worked in manufacturing shops where foul language was the norm. Having personally spent time in these types of environments, I know first-hand what goes on there. So, the difficulty in attempting to speak the truth in love is not as easy as it would appear under certain circumstances. Others simply expressed fear of the thought of confronting anyone for any reason. Few of us are good at anything the first time out, so overcoming fear requires courage and practice.

The overwhelming response to this thought of how to

challenge a person to stop speaking obscenities soon fell flat as the majority in the group admitted to using curse words daily, in their own lives. I reminded these men that they had once shared the sentiment of the desire to mentor young men. I asked them to think about the impression they would leave on young minds if they could not control their tongue. In worldly terms, the indisputable visible sign of a Christian would be the lack of curse words in our speech. Each of the men knew they needed to be more intentional with this most basic of qualities if they were ever going to leave the impression that they were followers of Jesus. Still, the thought of confronting the people in their work environment who used curse language loomed largely. I suggested that their focus should not be fear-based but presenting loving kindness. Instead of being fearful because of possible rejection or conflict, approach the men in love. Here is an example of what this conversation might look like:

"Joe, have you ever given much thought to the words you use? I've been looking at the world a little differently lately. It seems very dark. I wonder what the world will look like for my children and grandchildren. I realize that even in small ways, I can and should make changes. For instance, I have begun to examine my words, especially curse words. I realize that my I.Q. probably drops significantly when I use them. Because I use them so freely at work, I catch myself saying them at home in front of my wife and my children. I am not happy about that. I want to leave a different impression and certainly a different legacy for my family. Have you ever thought about that Joe? Would you consider holding me accountable for my words? I would be happy to return the favor. After all, I care about you and your family. What do you say? Are you in?"

In the example above, the narrator invites Joe into a meaningful conversation that has lasting implications. Instead of pointing a finger at Joe, thus making him defensive, the narrator involves himself and asks Joe if he would like to participate. In essence, a seed was planted which left Joe something to think about. If the narrator had already demonstrated that he could tame his tongue, the conversation above might look a little different. One of the most important things to remember about not being a "yes" man is that even though the advice is given, most times it won't be adhered to, at least in the initial instance. The only person who can change you is you. But that does not mean that we should not love that person enough to confront them. Once again, the idea of confronting a person is never something to be done flippantly. The depth of those types of conversations should be a direct reflection of the intimacy of the relationship. Do I know this person? Or do I only know *of* this person?

THE WORLD BECKONS

"The world and its desires pass away, but whoever does the will of God lives forever" (1 John 2:17). The world presses in on us from every side in ways that we are not aware of. We are being inundated continuously. When we are not aware, we are powerless to do anything about it. Not wanting to be a "yes" man might require us to remind those around us of the dangers that lurk. I often participate in men's retreats. This specific retreat was unique in the fact that you were asked to surrender all items of distraction upon entering the church, which would become home for four days. All clocks were removed from the walls. All watches, cell phones, computers, televisions, magazines, newspapers, etc. were also removed. At this retreat, 45 men were going to shut the world off, live in constant community, and sharpen each other through continuous study and learning of God. Oh, the depth of His grace!

Not always does the church, hosting the event, have the facilities to allow proper hygiene. At this church, there were no showers. However, the organizers had made arrangements for showers to be taken at a small gym less than a mile away.

At the end of the second day, some of the men elected to shower, while others waited until the middle of the third day. I was in the latter group of approximately 20. Upon arriving at the gym, I quickly realized these times were specific for a reason as no other patrons were around. As men were waiting their turn to shower, I began to hear words and witness behavior that can only be described as worldly. When I reminded everyone that we were Christian men on a retreat and that our conduct was always to be a witness for the Lord Jesus Christ, little changed.

After returning to the church, one of the older men who had been present at the gym approached me. During our conversation, he said something I have never forgotten. He said, "I am here to cram for my final exam." Based on his statement, I am unsure of the condition of his heart. Was his statement just a small glimpse of a bigger picture? It was not until after I returned home that God imparted the gravity of what had taken place. We were Christian men who had intentionally assembled and turned off the interruptions of the world to hear from God. After spending nearly 72 hours in complete seclusion, it took less than five minutes for the world to beckon us, and we bowed. I thought, how could this happen so easily?

Do we love people enough to never be their "yes" man?

4

PROMISE #3

I WILL ALWAYS POINT YOU TO JESUS

"**B**ut what about you?" he asked. "Who do you say I am?" Simon Peter answered, "You are the Messiah, the Son of the living God."' (Matthew 16:15-16).

Who is Jesus to you? Is He Lord and Savior? Is He the Way, the Truth, and the Life? Is He the only One in which salvation is found? Is He the only name under Heaven given to mankind by which we must be saved? Is He the Light that darkness could not diminish? Is He the Hope of Glory? Is He the divine self-expression of all that God is? Is He the One that we are to model our faith walk after?

My hope is your answer to every one of the previous questions is a resounding "YES!" Jesus is all those things and so much more. In fact, the word 'Savior' is mentioned only 36 times in the entire Bible. Conversely, the word 'Lord' appears more than 7,800 times. Why does the Word of God place such emphasis on 'Lord' over 'Savior?' Lord declares the position Jesus holds in your life, whereas Savior describes what He has done for you. We cannot partake of the benefit of His sacrifice unless we come under His position as Lord and King! We must spend our days on this earth pointing each other to Jesus.

The answer to every question....Jesus! Jesus + nothing = Everything! I hope I have made my point crystal clear.

GUARD AGAINST BIAS

Each of us has a bias inside us. This bias is based on our perspective of the world and life. This perspective is formed through the combination of our childhood, the time we spent with our parents, and the addition of our life experiences and other relationships. We need to remember this bias when we are leading the people God places in our lives. *"Therefore go and make disciples of all nations, baptizing them in the name of the Father and of the Son and of the Holy Spirit, and teaching them to obey everything I have commanded you. And surely I am with you always, to the very end of the age" (Matthew 28:19-20).* Clearly Jesus says teach them to obey what I have commanded you. This means we must never make disciples unto ourselves, but always point people to Jesus. Thus, we offer freely to people what we believe Jesus has given to us to give. In a later chapter, I will spend more time developing Truth #2 *"You Cannot Give Away What You Do Not Have."* For now, I want to spend some time thinking about how to guard against our natural bias'. Certainly, walking with others in both community and accountability will provide us with the framework we need to guard against our bias. If we are disciplined enough to self-examine, this can be an additional support in our endeavor to never make disciples unto ourselves.

BIAS EXERCISE

In one of my Chaplain trainings, we were given a test about perspective. This test was to help us see that there are multiple points of view (vantage points) in any circumstance, in fact, there could be as many points of view as there are people in the room. Would we remain teachable and willing to see the other points of view? Or would we believe only our vantage point contains perfect Truth? I have shared this story literally hundreds of times and each time the person hearing the story walks away with greater clarity. So, at the end of the story, I would like you, the reader, to point out which person is the most offensive to you. There is no right or wrong answer, as this is your perspective. There are only five characters and very few details.

This is the 5-Person Story: **A woman lived along a river. Her boyfriend lived on the other side. She wanted to visit, but there were no bridges. She finds a man with a boat and asks "Sir, would you take me across?" He answered, "For a night of sexual favors I will." The woman said, "No thank you." She approaches another man and asks, "Sir, would you help?" He responded, "I** would rather not get involved, thanks anyway." Feeling disappointed, she returned to the man with the boat, provided the sexual favors and he took her across the river. When her boyfriend heard of how she finally ended up on his side, he broke up with her. He did not like her choices. Feeling even more disappointment, the woman walked further along the river and found yet another man who later became her new boyfriend. When she revealed how she had arrived at his doorstep, the new boyfriend searched for, and found, the original boyfriend and beat him up for treating her so poorly.

Which of these characters is the most offensive to you? Why is this story helpful to us? If we are willing to see the biggest possible picture in any circumstance, the most points of view, it will help us not to be narrowly focused, solely on our particular point of view. Again, I ask, "why is this important?" If we are leading people from our particular point of view, in essence, we are asking people to think, act, and talk just like us instead of leading them to Christ. This cannot be! *"For what we preach is not ourselves, but Jesus Christ as Lord, and ourselves as your servants for Jesus' sake" (2 Corinthians 4:5).*

KNOW HIM

Of course, to lead people to Jesus, we must first have had our own personal encounter with Him. In thinking about who Jesus is in our lives, let's drawback to the beginning of this chapter. Is Jesus Lord of our lives? Are we pursuing Christ-likeness all our days? Some of us have convinced ourselves that He is, and we are. But all too often we find that most of us are content with Savior but not Lord. We live under the identity of "Christian" which provides the insurance policy, known as salvation, in which we place our hope. If Jesus were Lord, we might want to have a deep intimate relationship with Him. We would identify as 'follower" of Jesus. For many, this thought of knowing Jesus is scary because it might require something of us that we are not willing to relinquish. So, for a lot of us, we prefer Jesus as Savior only. This relationship is less intrusive, it plainly speaks of our willingness to know of Jesus, as opposed to our knowing Jesus. *"Not everyone who says to me, 'Lord, Lord,' will enter the kingdom of heaven, but only the one who does the will of my Father who is in heaven" (Matthew 7:21).*

For a long time, I was convinced that I was a person who

knew Jesus, until the day that I realized that I simply knew of Him. Like many other Christians, I committed my mornings to Bible study. Every day, I would devour page after page, consuming all that I could. This went on for many years. I probably read the Bible cover to cover five or more times. In my mind, everything seemed right. Then in 2011, I received a cancer diagnosis that required surgery. Upon returning home from the hospital, I found myself staring at my Bible desperately wanting to open it. During this time of physical healing, my Bible was right in front of me, every day. For six months I stared at it but could not open it. I was so confused and bewildered. Then one day while reading a book called "Knowing God" by J.I. Packer, I read this quote: **"For the fact that we have to face is this: If we pursue theological knowledge for its own sake, it is bound to go bad for us. It will make us proud and conceited. The very greatness of the subject matter will intoxicate us, and we shall come to think of ourselves as a cut above other Christians because of our interest in it; and we shall look down on those whose theological ideas seem to us crude and inadequate and dismiss them as poor specimens."** I was pierced to the core. I realized at that moment, that I may have some knowledge of Jesus, but I wasn't in a relationship with Jesus. If that were true, how could I know Jesus? If we are going to lead people to Jesus, we must know Him, not just know about Him. As my faith journey continues, I have come to the realization that the more I know of God and His Word, the less I know of God and His Word. The deeper I go to know Him the greater He becomes. There is one thing I know for sure; This life is not about us, it's all about Jesus!

BAPTISM

"For we were all baptized by one Spirit so as to form one body —whether Jews or Gentiles, slave or free—and we were all given the one Spirit to drink" (1 Corinthians 12:13). As the Scriptures remind us, we are all baptized in the same Spirit and form one body. Sometimes God will bring the most beautiful revelation to your mind and at a time least expected. A few years back, I attended a large crowd baptism that my church organizes once a year at a local metro park. The last person to be baptized that day was a man I had never met. As I watched Peter come up out of the water, he wept tears of joy which is not an uncommon reaction of the work of the Holy Spirit in us. What made me notice Peter's tears was his physical presence. Peter was a mountain of a man and extremely muscular. As we hugged, I thought, only the Holy Spirit could do such things. Peter shed tears of joy because he was made new.

The following year, I had no plans of attending the yearly baptism event because I had a previous commitment. Earlier that day, during church, I had been asked multiple times if I would be attending the baptism. Each time I answered, "no."

Then Mike, a man I disciple and also my previous commitment, informed me that he wanted to attend the baptism. I agreed to meet him there. Upon arriving, I stopped at the ice cream truck, which was parked at the edge of the grass, and got myself an ice cream.

While waiting for Mike, I decided to head to the prayer tent. The prayer leader shared that we needed to pray for the woman who was operating the ice cream truck as her husband had just died days earlier. I felt like God told me to go back to her truck and spend some time praying with her. God did this because I could offer her the comfort she needed. You see, just a few weeks earlier, I had lost a son. Our short meeting brought tears, joy, hope, and a bit of healing for both of us. I remember walking away thanking God for allowing me to be His vessel.

I then found my way down to the front, near the water. I began to speak to a couple of our church officials. I asked if they recalled Peter's baptism from the previous year, and how special it was? They both agreed it was amazing. And just then Peter walked right past me. I politely excused myself and approached Peter. We had built a small bond over the year since his baptism, and I wanted to spend some intentional time with him and strengthen that bond. Peter agreed.

I returned to the church officials and I shared with them the irony that came with this moment. Nearly 15 years earlier, I had been baptized in the same water. But it almost didn't happen. "Why," they asked? I was working out of town and making arrangements to appear in Detroit for the large crowd baptism the next day. While on my laptop, I opened an email that was laced with porn. Sadly, it took me practically 15 minutes to come to my senses. As I sat in my hotel room, I began to question how I was going to be able to get baptized the next day. I truly felt sick inside.

At that moment, I received a call from Mitch (not sharing

his real name for privacy), the friend who ushered me through the salvation prayer about three years earlier. Mitch felt like God told him to call me and I shared with him what had just happened. God always sends the right people! To this, Mitch said that God loves me and has great plans for me. He assured me that I was to be baptized the next day and although he could not be in attendance, he was expecting a phone call to hear all about it. After sharing this with the church officials, they were astonished and said, "God is so amazing! Only God could orchestrate all the events necessary for Mitch to call you at the moment when you needed encouragement the most. ABSOLUTELY AMAZING!"

After leaving the church officials, I spent some time praying with many of the individuals who were about to be baptized. Shortly after the baptism ceremony started, rain began to fall. When the rain became a monsoon, the whole crowd was partaking in the baptism, literally. I found shelter underneath the prayer tent where the night began. It was there that I found Mike, the person I had come to meet. While watching the baptism and sharing some small talk, the rain suddenly stopped and the skies cleared as if the rain had never come, leaving no trace. At that moment, Mitch, the man who ushered me through the salvation prayer, Mitch who randomly called me the night before my baptism almost 15 years earlier, Mitch who told me that God loved me and had great plans for me, Mitch a man I had not seen in almost 20 years, that Mitch walked right in front of me. I yelled, "Mitch!" "What are you doing here?" He recognized me and we embraced in a hug. Mitch asked how my family was doing? I was paralyzed with silence. I wanted to answer his question, but at the same time, I did not want to burden him with the weight of my son's death at our first encounter in nearly 20 years. He could tell there was something amiss and stated that he had to run but was so thankful to see me.

When I got in my car to return home that evening, I had an unsettled spirit. I felt like I needed to reach out to Mitch and explain why I had acted strangely. I was surprised to find his name still on my phone and even more surprised when he answered. We spoke at length and got caught up in each other's lives. Today, Mitch and I maintain steady contact.

IMMEASURABLY MORE

"Now to him who is able to do immeasurably more than all we ask or imagine, according to his power that is at work within us" (Ephesians 3:20). How could all these events have lined up in this way on a single night? What if Mike had not wanted to attend the baptism? What if I had not gone to the prayer tent? What if I had not spoken to the church officials? What if I had not run into Peter? What if it hadn't rained that night? What if Mitch hadn't called me in my hotel room years earlier? What if Mitch hadn't convinced me that God loved me and that I was meant to be baptized? What if Mitch had never pointed me to Jesus all those years ago? Would I have written this book? Would you be reading this book? It's not about us. It's all about Jesus.

To love your neighbor well, offer them Promise #3, *"I Will Always Point You To Jesus!"*

5

PROMISE #4

I WILL ALWAYS HAVE OPEN ARMS READY
TO RECEIVE YOU

Promise #4, *"I Will Always Have Open Arms Ready To Receive You"* takes on greater depth if Promise #1, *"I Will Never Judge You"* is effectively displayed. Without the first promise, there may never be any follow up. Sometimes we only get one opportunity, a few brief moments, or a chance encounter to leave this impression of Jesus with people. What I have learned from my own journey is that people do return, when they are ready, if they don't feel rejection and if they know that our love is abundant. If we push people away, if we are not present *in* the moment, if we don't make them feel like their circumstances are the most important thing going on in that moment, if we're callous with their vulnerability, if we reduce them to a number, if we look past them as if they were invisible, then we become agents of alienation. If we saddled any person with any of those things, why would they ever come back?

Rejection always dissolves any hope of trust and removes the possibility of a relationship. As with anything else that we do, including the principles outlined in this book, we get good at what we practice. We can always become better at receiving people and showering our neighbor with love like our Father in Heaven does for us. *"So he got up and went to his father. But while he was still a long way off, his father saw him and was filled with compassion for him; he ran to his son, threw his arms around him and kissed him" (Luke 15:20).*

AT A DISTANCE

Before we can learn how to love our neighbor, we must first shed our belief that we are "good" apart from God. If we want to give the love of God to others, we must rely on Him and receive His love. God is the Source! Apart from Him, we can only present a love we have manufactured from our flesh which might resemble love, but all too often feels like *favor* to the recipient. In a later chapter, we will discuss in greater depth Truth #2, *"You Cannot Give Away What You Do Not Have."* For now, let us concentrate on the fact that we need Jesus, or we cannot love. *"As it is written: **There is no one righteous, not even one; there is no one who understands; there is no one who seeks God. All have turned away, they have together become worthless; there is no one who does good, not even one"** (Romans 3:10-12).*

When do we realize that God is the Author of all things? When do we turn to Him as our Source? I remember, before I became a follower of Christ, when I learned this truth the hard way. God sends people into our lives and we are unaware of the roles they play. Sometimes they plant seeds for future harvest and sometimes they turn our eyes to the Lord. Sam was a friend of mine. He wasn't like my real friend, but sort of a friend of a friend. We would spend some time together, but only when Dave was among us. Dave was the link to our connection. Sam was sometimes strange, sometimes weird, and had some odd behaviors. For this reason, I kept him at a distance. Sam was also kind and funny and generous, but I knew what I was doing. After all, I was a good person. Isn't that what we tell ourselves?

How many of us have lived in this space? On occasion, I still have to fight myself from reclaiming that space once again. Sam and I lived exactly one-quarter mile from each other. Still, much time had escaped us, and I paid him no mind. One day, Sam came down with a cold, so I was told. After Sam's wife grew tired of hearing his cough, she asked him to go to the doctor and get a penicillin shot. Sam never returned home again. Small-Cell Lung Cancer took his life three weeks from that doctor visit. I visited Sam in the hospital, and would you believe I still looked past him. Don't get me wrong I felt bad and acted as if I cared, but the truth is I was consumed with other things more important than Sam. I stayed in the waiting room with his wife and kids for a couple of hours to convince them, and myself, that Sam was important to me.

While attending the funeral, something strange began to happen as I was overcome with emotion. Guilt, fear, worry, and regret were just a few of the emotions I was experiencing, along with many tears. The next day I woke up and had this strong pull to go to the store and purchase a Bible. That was the day my journey with the Lord began. Although I did not know God yet, I had a strange desire to want to. I have never forgotten Sam and I am certain I never will. When I get to Heaven, he is a person I am hoping to find. I will thank him in person for the gift that he gave me, especially after I treated him so poorly. This time, however, instead of keeping him at a distance, I will have open arms ready to receive him.

GUARDIANS OF HIS HONOR

Do we actually believe what the Scriptures say? If we say we do, why does it take a life-shattering event before most of us are willing to turn our eyes to Him? Why are we more like the expert in the law, from Luke 10, who asked "Who is my neighbor?" Why do we continue to act like someone who wants to be a counselor to Jesus instead of walking in obedience? *"Follow God's example, therefore, as dearly loved children" (Ephesians 5:1).* If God created each of us in His image and if we are all His children, perhaps we should begin to study His character and follow His example?

Here are a few things to ponder. First, are we thankful that God entrusts us with the responsibility to be guardians of His honor? No matter what we have done, no matter where we have been, no matter how many times we have fallen, God trusts us to safeguard His honor as His sons and daughters. Do we consider any meeting with any person a privilege? Are we willing to look at any person in the way that God looks at us? Must we be reminded that the person in front of us is also someone for whom Christ died? Do we cultivate an attitude of *awe*? Do we admire? Do we respect?

Are we amazed at the assembly God has arranged for us? No? Perhaps we should?

If love *"always"* protects, *"always"* trusts, *"always"* hopes, *"always"* perseveres, and *"never"* fails then why are there still so many Sam's in the world? We must be willing to make even the smallest difference in our own spheres of influence. Without God, we can't and without us, He won't! Promising to always have open arms to receive people challenges us with many questions. I will ask only one more. Which one of us would reject a reception that made us feel that we are the most valuable person, that we matter, that we are loved and that we are accepted without exception? When any person is confronted with God's agape (complete, all-encompassing, perfect) love, they will return over and over and over again.

WHEN YOU LEAST EXPECT IT

"Do nothing out of selfish ambition or vain conceit. Rather, in humility value others above yourselves, not looking to your own interests but each of you to the interests of the others. In your relationships with one another, have the same mindset as Christ Jesus" (Philippians 2:3-5). A wise man once told me that God works in the gaps. Sometimes we don't recognize what He's doing. His ways are higher! Sometimes we are received with open arms and don't see it coming. It's not until much later, when our vision becomes much clearer, that we appreciate the person(s) God would place in our life. It's only then, after this person becomes more than a friend, more than a brother, more than a mentor that you realize he modeled Promise #4, *"I Will Always Have Open Arms Ready To Receive You"* in the gap.

I was feeling led to participate in a ministry at my church. During the training season of this ministry, the leaders paired people together, thus making us prayer partners. This pairing was also to provide additional support and a sense of greater community. In my group, there was an odd number of men and when we drew names, I drew the short straw. The leadership team decided that one of them would step in to fill this role as my prayer partner. When Al called me the first time, neither of us knew what would become of our relationship. Our conversations and prayers not only brought us closer together but drew us closer to God as well. Weeks turned to months and months turned to years. Today we have been entwined for more than 10 years and God continues to be the focus. In fact, you might even call our relationship 'providential.'

There is no way Al could have known what God was going to do. I am certain that Al was not even aware of Promise #4, *"I Will Always Have Open Arms Ready To Receive You."* What I do know is this, God wastes nothing. Every moment of our life He will use for His glory. Everything is preparation for what is to come. Because of Al's obedience to the Lord, he modeled something valuable for me. Al's focus was not on me, his focus was on God. God allowed me to experience something so treasured that I would put it into practice in my own life, and now I share it with you.

BY THE PRINCIPLE OR BY THE SPIRIT?

We live in a world where there is limited margin. We are always striving to get to the next thing. Our calendars are full, and we boast of how busy we are. We are human beings, but we act more like human doings. Where can we find a safe harbor? Where do we find a person who will receive us and simply just be "with" us? Where is this person who will press zero demands upon us and allow us the space to vent our frustrations? Where is the person who will talk with us about anything and never judge us? Where is the person who will not force us into a theological conversation, but simply be a friend in a spiritual context? *"So I say, walk by the Spirit, and you will not gratify the desires of the flesh. For the flesh desires what is contrary to the Spirit, and the Spirit what is contrary to the flesh. They are in conflict with each other, so that you are not to do whatever you want" (Galatians 5:16-17).*

I recall a conversation I once had with a friend of mine concerning the idea of what it looks like to live either by the principle or by the Spirit. He said that living by the principle will serve us well most of the time and that many people endorse this method. Living by the principle convinces us that we are organized and loving. Our calendars are neatly outlined with each of our daily meetings, and we are certain to give each person our utmost attention. Except, somewhere between meeting number three and meeting number four arrives a person we weren't expecting to encounter. If we are living by the principle, we may not see them. If we don't see them, we may not step into their circumstances. If we don't step into their circumstances, we most certainly won't receive them with open arms. However, if we are living by the Spirit, we will most definitely see them, and we might just step into their circumstances, and possibly receive them with open arms. In fact, if we are living by the Spirit, we may go as far as canceling the remaining six meetings we had neatly planned on our calendars for that day, especially if their circumstances are crucial. We would do this because we recognize that God brought this person into our path so we could demonstrate His love and shine His light.

Do we always recognize the people God brings to us? No! Even when we see them, do we always step into their circumstances? No! But there is one thing I am sure of; we get good at what we practice. Let us grow in our faith and become more aware of those around us. In doing so, we can receive every person with open arms and experience greater joy.

REALLY GOD?

"Now that you have purified yourselves by obeying the truth so that you have sincere love for each other, love one another deeply, from the heart" (1 Peter 1:22). The journey to receiving people with open arms can sometimes take unexpected twists. We often dupe ourselves into believing we have "entered" into understanding all that love requires. We have revered such a variety of God's people that we lull ourselves into false maturity. It is in these moments, fleeting as they might be, that we think of ourselves as being better than others. When we do this, we have done a very foolish thing. However, it is in these moments that God can humble us and reveal new depths of His love.

It was the day of my son Michael's funeral. The pain of suffering is a guest to many as suffering is a part of our fallen world. The day of a child's funeral is when suffering becomes a permanent resident to the parent. No words can ever adequately describe the vacuum of this darkness. As I stood at the doorway greeting person after person for nearly six hours, I was grateful for the outpouring of support. At various times prior to the service, some of the people needed *me* to minister to *them*. When the first person came along, I thought, how could this be? I was lost in my emotions, grieving my son, trying to keep it all together. I needed comforting and yet I was being asked to comfort others on one of the worst days of my life. I remember asking, "Really God? This is what You want?" "Okay God, I'll do it."

Each time this happened I remember experiencing an increased sense of loneliness. After several of these moments, I stopped questioning God. It was then that loneliness left me, and comfort overwhelmed me. It was as though God had placed His hand on my shoulder and said, "I am right here by your side. I have never left you. We will get through this together. I know exactly how hard this is for you. Now you have a greater understanding of how wide and long and high and deep my love is for you. My son, you can now reach more people as my vessel to expand My Kingdom and glorify My name." In the first calendar year after my son's death, God placed me in front of 17 men who had also lost sons. I received them all with open arms!

FATHER, THANK YOU FOR YOUR INFINITE MERCY. THANK YOU FOR BEARING WITH ME AND BELIEVING IN ME, ESPECIALLY WHEN I GET FRUSTRATED WITH THE CLASH OF MY FLESH. PULL ME CLOSER AND IMPART TO ME THIS SAME GRACE AND MERCY SO I MAY POUR IT OUT TO OTHERS. YOUR LOVE IS AMAZING. MAY EVERYONE I ENCOUNTER EXPERIENCE YOU.

6

TRUTH #1

ONCE YOU LEARN A NEW "TRUTH," YOU CANNOT UNLEARN IT

W e've probably all heard at least one person say that they are "set in their ways" or "you can't teach an old dog new tricks." These types of thoughts tend to permeate many people's thinking and cause them to resist anything new. This type of thinking is fear-based and if we are not careful can keep us trapped forever. Our thought life is very important because as Scripture would remind us, "as a man thinks, so a man does." So, if a person is set in his/her ways, there is probably very little chance that he/she is open-minded.

If you are attempting to become an expert in anything, there will always be something new to learn. Therefore, the first step in learning something new is the willingness to entertain new thoughts. Whether you believe it or not, listening to another person's perspective is, in fact, showing love to that person. It's not enough to simply listen to new thoughts, we must also be willing to apply those thoughts to our daily lives. This is especially important when those thoughts are beneficial to our lives; when they are "truths" that God has preserved for us. *"Do not merely listen to the word, and so deceive yourselves. Do what it says"* *(James 1:22).* Because of technology, there has never been a time in history when we have had access to more information than we do today. Unfortunately, the opposite can also be said; there has never been a time when society, as a whole, has been more unknowing.

This is why Truth #1, *"Once You Learn A New "Truth," You Cannot Unlearn It,"* is so vital and why I believe it's a major part of God's command of loving your neighbor as yourself. We should never stop learning. We should always believe we can continue to learn. Since the ability to learn is a truth, we should always desire to learn.

DISCIPLESHIP

"And the things you have heard me say in the presence of many witnesses entrust to reliable people who will also be qualified to teach others" (2 Timothy 2:2). This passage in 2 Timothy provides a framework in which we are to share information with others. It clearly states that there must be an exchange, someone willing to give, and someone willing to receive. Jesus commanded us to make disciples of all nations, therefore we must be willing to share with others. Furthermore, that also means we must be willing to learn and discover new truths ourselves. Sometimes these truths have already been established in the understanding of our minds. As we grow in faith, we can discern greater meaning to the truths already uncovered as well as establish new ones.

The best way to foster this type of discovery is through discipleship. I had already been discipling or mentoring, men for several years when I was graced by God to meet my mentor and friend Loren. Loren has spent more than 40 years not only being discipled but also discipling others. Through his guidance, I have been able to glean new understanding and to become more aware of how God was leading me as a husband, father, friend, brother, son, and leader. Loren has taught me that we must always learn, that there is always more and that we will never exhaust the depth of God. Because of my encounter with Loren, which I believe was predestined by God, I have been able to share many new truths with the men that I disciple. Just as the verse above indicates, the men that God has placed in my life now share new truths with the men God places in their lives. Leading by example is a truth in itself. True discipleship can only come by way of example. Discipleship was something designed by God, but regrettably, much of mankind has deemed this method of learning new truths as unimportant. Men have justified this position by stating that they already know what to do or they simply just don't need help or don't want help. However, the proof of our "knowing" it is in our "living" it. Sadly, one can reason that the majority of the problems in society today are the direct result of men turning their backs on this time-honored truth called discipleship.

Some of the biggest setbacks in our society, due to the disregard of God, ultimately affect our families. When the Bible speaks of generational curses, it is referring to the behaviors, or practices, that we leave behind such as divorce, addiction, selfishness, and of course the removal of God in our homes. Discipleship can help *illuminate* these behaviors and bring about change as we apply new truths to our lives. With the help of our mentors who walk beside us and live as an example to follow, we can change the legacy that we leave to our loved ones. Hence, loving your neighbor as yourself is developed in our relationships through discipleship.

H2O SOCIETY

Another major obstacle that we must learn to overcome is the idea that we can achieve something of value by exerting minimal effort. Today, we are encouraged to take the easiest route possible, settle for the way things are, leave everything to chance, follow the crowd, put things off, and even to ignore people instead of loving them and forgiving them. I like to refer to our current society as the H_2O Society because water always takes the path of least resistance in any circumstance. We, humans, have fortified this principle as a way of life, and it consumes everything we do. We must reject this notion because it is of no value. *"Enter through the narrow gate. For wide is the gate and broad is the road that leads to destruction, and many enter through it. But small is the gate and narrow the road that leads to life, and only a few find it"* *(Matthew 7:13-14).*

Unfortunately, what we regularly find, in many parts of the world, is the idea of reducing discipleship into this same thought of H_2O's least resistance. Discipleship must never be condensed into a formula or a process or a set of procedures. The truth behind discipleship is not completing some tasks and then graduating into something that is now able to do the same but to live in a relationship with those who would walk with you as you live a life that is dedicated to the obedience of the command of Christ Jesus. For this reason, there can never be an arrangement of a pre-determined outcome. Eugene Peterson, author of "Working the Angles" shares this quote, **"It is easier to tell people what to do than to be with them in a discerning, prayerful companionship as they work it out. But the very nature of the life of faith requires the personal and the immediate if we are going to mature: not only wisdom but a wise person to understand us in relation to the wisdom. A person in need and in growth is vulnerable and readily accepts counsel that is sincerely given. But the help that might be right for someone else, even right for this person at another time, can be wrong for this person at this time. So the congregations need for personal spiritual direction cannot be delegated to books, or tapes or videos. It is the pastors proper work."**

The truth of discipleship begins with a personal relationship. Just as each person is uniquely different, so is the relationship of discipleship. Each person begins in a different place, each person retains information at a different rate, each person has a different set of life experiences, and each person has a different level of understanding. We who are discipling must learn to walk "with" people and at their pace. If we are in front, we are pulling and if we are in back, we are pushing. If we are pulling or pushing, we are not loving our neighbor, we are simply attempting to create results. The results are never ours; they are always Gods.

CHOICES

"If any of you lacks wisdom, you should ask God, who gives generously to all without finding fault, and it will be given to you" (James 1:5). How many times do we have to be reminded that our choices are important? The choices make leave a lasting effect on virtually every person we encounter, especially those closest to us. Probably the most important choice we will ever make is to turn to Jesus Christ and to give our lives to Him. Waiting until tomorrow to live for Christ is waiting too long. For through this one choice, comes understanding, purpose, and calling. The choice to follow Christ can totally transform our lives and bring enlightenment of all Truth and remove the arrogance and pride that lives in each person. We must remove ourselves as counselors of God and our propensity to reason against Him.

"Every scholar, every disputer of this world, nay, every man, has been where Eve was, and has done what she did, when she sought for wisdom that did not come from God. All libraries of the world are the full proof of the remaining power of the first sinful thirst after it: they are full of the knowledge that comes not from God, and

therefore, proceeds from that first fountain of subtlety that opened her eyes. For as there cannot possibly be any goodness in man, but so far as the divine goodness is living and working good in Him, so that there cannot be any divine truth, or knowledge in man, but so far as God's truth and knowledge is opened, living and working in him, because God alone is truth, and the knowledge of it" (The Power of the Spirit by William Law).

The encouragement to seek the wisdom of God is found in His Word. In it are the truths for right living. When our relationship with God is central, every other relationship finds greater depth and bears importance. Our lives are no longer primary to us but serving God and serving others becomes most important. We no longer compare ourselves with anyone else, but instead look at people through His eyes, in love. We become teachable and allow God to fashion us into what He created us to be. We begin to bear the fruit of the Spirit and thus learn to truly love our neighbor as ourselves.

THE DAPHNE PROJECT

"As man's obedience increases, his actions decrease. When we first begin to follow the Lord, we are full of activity but quite short of obedience. But as we advance in spirituality our actions gradually diminish until we are filled with obedience. Many, however, do what they like and refuse to do what they dislike. They never ponder whether or not they are acting out of obedience. Hence many works are done out of self and not in obedience to God" (Author unknown). Living out the truth of walking in obedience to God is a continuous journey of discovery. As we become more about Him and less about us, we begin to see His promptings more clearly.

A friend of mine was coordinating a weeklong service project, in a neighboring community, which she labeled the "Daphne Project." Daphne had evidently made some wonderful contributions to society and my friend Barb wanted to bless her because of it. I grabbed a couple of men from my church and we showed up to help paint. While at the Daphne Project, Barb shared that there was a cancelation in the upcoming mission trip to Texas, and she wanted me to fill the spot since I had traveled with her group many times previously. Barb also stated that the departure date was less than two weeks away. Still, I agreed. Before leaving the Daphne Project that day, I asked if we could meet Daphne, but was informed that she was not in town.

On the way home, I decided to visit my aunt. Nothing could prepare me for what I was about to find. When I arrived, I found my cousin dead on the front porch. Serving as a Chaplain, I have sat with many people as they took their last breath. But this experience was closer to home as it was my family. In all the confusion, with the police and the detectives, I had almost forgotten about the mission trip I had just agreed to be a part of. With all the arrangements that are necessary for planning a 10-day trip, coupled with a family funeral in which I would perform the service, I was leaning toward canceling the mission trip simply because time was not in my favor. Instead, I persisted as my schedule allowed.

The mission trip was long, and the heat in Texas was nearly unbearable. Unlike the other trips I had been on previously, this one had a lack of resources and organization. Each day brought more challenges than the one before. I started talking to God and asking, "Why am I here God? Ever since I agreed to come on this trip there has been one struggle after the next. This trip is nothing like my previous experiences." I kept asking God these questions each day. *"And we know that in all things God works for the good of those who love him, who have been called according to his purpose" (Romans 8:28).*

Finally, the end of the week came. Two other groups joined us on that final day, in hopes we might complete our work on the house we were assigned. Before leaving that home, all three groups joined hands in prayer to thank God for choosing us to be His vessels. At that moment a woman, who I did not know, began to cry and fell to her knees. I approached her to console and minister to her. She said she was overwhelmed with gratitude for all that God had done. I asked her name so I could pray for her. She said, "My name is Daphne." If this would have been the same Daphne from the beginning of the story it would be even more incredible. How many people are named Daphne? Nevertheless, I was speechless! I thought, "God, how did you do this?" From the time that I appeared at the Daphne Project until that moment of prayer, I had experienced three weeks of continuous trials and many times almost did not continue. After some time of reflection, I realized that God wanted my obedience. It was as if He was asking, "How far would you go and what would you be willing to endure to pray for a woman named Daphne, on my behalf?" If we are going to love our neighbor, we must learn that obedience is key.

COME AND GET YOUR BOOK

It's been my experience that God will use just about anything to gain our attention. He wants our obedience more than anything. If we want to be obedient to God, we must learn to be present *in* the moment. If we are not present *in* the moment, we will never learn to love our neighbor because to love someone is to be "with" them. Far too often, we get in front of God and He will use whatever means necessary to correct our posture. Let us never forget the truth of being present *in* the moment so we can grow in our understanding of how to best love our neighbor. ***"Therefore do not worry about tomorrow, for tomorrow will worry about itself. Each day has enough trouble of its own" (Matthew 6:34).***

It was the last day of a three-day leadership summit and I was thinking about all that I needed to accomplish after it concluded. I decided that I would leave the summit a little early to ensure that I had enough time to stop at the funeral home to visit my friend Al before meeting a man who was interested in a mentoring relationship. Both stops were on opposite sides of town. As I was saying goodbye to my friends, and making my way out of the summit, I heard my name announced from the stage. My first reaction was that I did not have time for this. I was anxious and fearful that I had left zero margin for error in the remainder of my day. Then the voice from the stage stated that I had been selected as the winner of a book and I needed to come to the stage to retrieve it. My mind was racing at this point. I was thinking that we never get a second chance to leave the first impression and how would I ever get to my last meeting on time. So, I quickly grabbed the book and immediately left.

On the way to the funeral home, my anxiety was heightened as construction was delaying my commute. Of course, the parking lot of the funeral home was jam-packed, and it took a bit to find a spot to park. I found my friend amid a very crowded room. He began to share an amazing story about his now deceased, estranged brother. Al was humbled by the discovery of who his brother actually was and the way he lived his life because it was vastly different from what he had thought. It seemed his brother was more like Christ Jesus than few had given him credit for. But instead of being deterred by the naysayers, Al's brother continued to glorify God with his life. Al was thankful, both for the life his brother had led and for the stretching of his faith knowing that he, too, had been one to give little regard for his brother. But Al wasn't done yet. Because of his brother's death, Al now had to interact with his father who he had not spoken to in over 30 years. He proceeded to share a story of redemption and restoration and humility and forgiveness and healing. We both shed many tears rejoicing at what God had done. But now I had to leave to ensure I would make my last appointment.

I rushed to the other side of town and arrived with five minutes to spare. To my surprise, the man I was to meet that day never showed. After inquiring, it appeared that our days got crossed and we were not meeting until the following week. On the drive home, God revealed to me that I was so concerned with my last meeting of the day that I almost forgot to be present in all the moments before it. He then reminded me that a book, won at a leadership conference, slowed me down long enough so I could eventually enter a crowded funeral home, be uninterrupted, and hear two marvelous stories that only God could design. God is amazing! Life happens *in* the moment and *in* the moment is where we love our neighbor.

Let us embrace the idea that new truths are revealed to us constantly by God. He is drawing us closer with each passing moment. We may not understand fully today but His Truth is like His Word, sweeter than honey. *"For now we see only a reflection as in a mirror; then we shall see face to face. Now I know in part; then I shall know fully, even as I am fully known" (1 Corinthians 13:12).*

7

TRUTH #2

YOU CANNOT GIVE AWAY WHAT YOU DO NOT HAVE

Truth #2, *"You Cannot Give Away What You Do Not Have"* seems simple, and it is. It's us who make simple statements complicated. We do this because we want to decide and be in charge of every outcome.

I remember having a conversation with a very wise man after a Bible study on this very topic. The wise man began to argue with me because he thought Truth #2 was flawed. I said, "You are overcomplicating it, just take it as it is." He continued to argue. I asked him how much cash he had with him? "Forty-seven dollars", he replied. To which I stated, "I need fifty dollars. Can you give it to me?" He finally submitted to the truth and simplicity of the statement. Seeing this truth clearly, impacts virtually every exchange we have with those whom God allows to grace our paths.

Every person has the ability to give what they have, but they cannot give away more than this. This does not mean that we should be afraid to offer whatever we may have to give in the moment but be aware of the limits of our offering. This includes grace, love, joy, peace, patience, kindness, goodness, faithfulness, gentleness, and self-control. You can give to the measure you have of these attributes, but nothing more. You cannot listen more intently, forgive more fully, nor can you understand more deeply. Neither can you advise, instruct, or counsel on matters unfamiliar to you. What if we have never been discipled? Can we disciple others? I would argue not well. What if we are not living out our faith openly and authentically? Would we be able to make disciples as we are commanded? Thankfully, with God, there is always more. Every circumstance, every trial, every tribulation, every success brings a new perspective and therefore more to give away. What we can give away is based on what exudes from our soul in the present moment. Each encounter also brings with it, the ability to love our neighbor more in the same way that God loves us. We can only give away the measure of love we have received from Him. *"But grow in the grace and knowledge of our Lord and Savior Jesus Christ. To him be glory both now and forever! Amen" (2 Peter 3:18).*

IS IT VALUABLE TO YOU?

Our faith and obedience to God should be of utmost importance to us. Every Christian is called by God to be an influencer in the world and to those around them. Scripture tells us that we should be Holy and set apart and refers to believers as the *salt* and *light* of the world. Salt has two purposes. First, *salt* is used to enhance flavor. Second, *salt* is used as a preservative. So, our Christian demonstration adds flavor to our faith. Our transformed lives equally demonstrate the preservative power of the gospel.

The *light* we reflect is not our own as it comes from God. It says that we witness to the world the Truth of God's Word, who Christ is, and of the resurrection. We do this through awareness, knowledge, and understanding. *"You are the salt of the earth. But if the salt loses its saltiness, how can it be made salty again? It is no longer good for anything, except to be thrown out and trampled underfoot. You are the light of the world. A town built on a hill cannot be hidden. Neither do people light a lamp and put it under a bowl. Instead they put it on its stand, and it gives light to everyone in the house. In the same way, let your light shine before others, that they may see your good deeds and glorify your Father in heaven" (Matthew 5:13-16).* If your faith is not valuable to you, it won't be valuable to anyone else. If God entrusts us with such a wonderful responsibility, perhaps we should take Him and His Word seriously? Let us live authentic faith-driven lives and then we will be able to give the love of God away to all.

OUT OF YOUR OVERFLOW

One of the basic principles that I have been taught through my discipleship experience is the idea that we must learn to live in faith each day out of our overflow. How do we do this and why is it important? Some of the basic tenets of our faith include daily prayer, worship, Bible reading, Bible studies, the fellowship of believers, church attendance, and discipleship relationships. All of these practices can and will bring us closer to the knowledge and power of the Holy Spirit. *"May the God of hope fill you with all joy and peace as you trust in him, so that you may overflow with hope by the power of the Holy Spirit" (Romans 15:13).* Why is this important? Each of us has been given authority by God and is required to steward well the influence that we have been given.

Daily there will be people who need something from us. They include our spouse, our children, our parents, our friends, our co-workers, and the acquaintances that we encounter each day. The things we offer might be as simple as a kind word, a hug, a listening ear, encouragement, a ten-dollar bill, or even advice. If our cup is full and overflowing with the fruit of the Spirit, we always have something valuable and *fresh* to offer to each person because we are full ourselves.

What happens if we discontinue filling ourselves? We may be able to function on some tolerable level for a time, but slowly our cup will begin to empty. This emptying, or distancing from God, is not noticeable to the naked eye. One day we wake up and everything is suddenly different, and we are unsure how we got there. We may still be able to provide the necessary things that our loved ones require, that is until we are completely empty. However, if an emergency were to arise, anything valuable would quickly evaporate. Instead of approaching us on an individual basis, an emergency would bring multiple people at the same time until the crisis subsided. If these people needed grace, mercy, love, patience, kindness, discernment, or wisdom we would end up offering them just the opposite. Without an overflow of the Holy Spirit, our offering might include anger, anxiety, worry, impatience, and harshness. It would be impossible to love our neighbor if this is what we extended to people. Let us remember, you cannot give away what you do not have.

I HAVE A LICENSE

Suffering exists in every person's life in different measures and in different seasons. We will never escape suffering as it is part of life. In fact, longsuffering is a fruit of the Spirit. Many of us will encounter opportunities to minister to people who are in the center of pronounced suffering and in huge need of comfort. Too often, these exchanges are handled inappropriately because most of us attempt, with good intentions I would add, to offer more than we have. Often, we find ourselves in very uncomfortable circumstances and experience awkward moments of silence. As a result, we begin to fill the silence with words. Those words, although meant to be soothing and provide support, often leave those suffering in greater want. We can learn a great deal about loving our neighbor in these uncomfortable moments by not avoiding them. As we navigate our faith journey and experience our own suffering, God will bring to us, those who have received His comfort through similar circumstances, who can then comfort us. Each time this happens we are left with *more* to give away. *"Praise be to the God and Father of our Lord Jesus*

Christ, the Father of compassion and the God of all comfort, who comforts us in all our troubles, so that we can comfort those in any trouble with the comfort we ourselves receive from God" (2 Corinthians 1:3-4).

It was the day of my son Michael's funeral, arguably the worst day for any parent. I remember a numbness overwhelming me and looking at the world through tears. I thought, "Could this really be happening? Will I wake up from this horrible nightmare?" In the middle of the day, my phone vibrated with an unfamiliar number. I don't know why I decided to read it at that moment, but I did. The message was brief, but crystal clear at the same time. It read, "My name is Hank. I have a license to talk to you. Today I begin praying for you. I am so sorry for what you are experiencing. When you're ready, I will be here for you." Upon reading this text, I immediately knew I wasn't alone. Somebody else, who I did not know, had lost a son and was reaching out to provide support. Believe it or not, this text brought great comfort to me. After some time had passed, I met with Hank and we shared our experiences over coffee. I am confident that both of us are healthier for this encounter.

As God would have it, I, too, would be provided many opportunities to bless others with the encouragement I received from Hank. At the time of writing this book, nearly 13 months after my son's death, I have encountered 19 men who have lost sons. I have often reflected and sat in prayer wondering what I was supposed to take away from all of this. What did God want me to know? Then one day, I recalled two funerals I performed some years ago for parents who had lost sons. During those services, I remember stating to these devastated parents, that my words will fall short. Instead, I would pray they encounter someone who had experienced such tragedy as they had and who had learned to engage life once again. These were the people who could offer the most comfort, the most understanding, and the most hope because they had walked in their shoes. After this reflection, I realized that I had become what I prayed for those parents. I had something more to give to a suffering world.

SOME MEASURE OF
UNDERSTANDING

Sometimes God will place us in challenging and difficult circumstances that will test not only our obedience to Him and our willingness to love our neighbor but also our awareness that we cannot give away what we do not have. In these moments, we discover that loving our neighbor is not always the easiest thing to do. *"If you love those who love you, what reward will you get? Are not even the tax collectors doing that?" (Matthew 5:46).*

I remember receiving an email from the church with a request to make a house visit for the last rites of a loved one. I quickly called the number and asked if it was necessary to come that day or could it wait until the morning. The voice on the phone was anxious and hurried, and although I did not clearly understand what she was saying, I knew I had to arrive that day. God told me to call a friend of mine, Debbie, to go along. She was a fellow Chaplain and had been on these types of calls numerous times. It is always better to take another person just to keep the protocol and maintain integrity.

Upon arriving, we sat with the woman whom I had called, along with her two daughters, and began to talk. She explained her mother's condition was dire, which was why she wanted us to arrive that evening. Her mother was in hospice care in her bedroom across the hall. She also expressed anger at how she was handled by the church. She felt like her needs were not important and wanted to know why she had to speak to so many people before I finally contacted her. She had a strong accent which made communicating a little difficult and this was probably why she ended up being transferred to a couple of different people when she called the church. Between her accent, anxiousness, and her hurried voice, the receptionist probably had a difficult time understanding her desires. I assured her that she was important and that her church was present to take care of her needs. She appeared to calm down.

Very often, people who are dying, and sometimes even their loved ones, can become distraught with thoughts about what is next. They begin to ask this question, "How do we know we will go to Heaven?" In this example, the family asked us to perform the last rites. Debbie and I knew that there was nothing that we could do to guarantee this woman's passage into Heaven. If she had never asked Jesus as her Lord and Savior, we could certainly lead her in this prayer. *'If you declare with your mouth, "Jesus is Lord," and believe in your heart that God raised him from the dead, you will be saved. For it is with your heart that you believe and are justified, and it is with your mouth that you profess your faith and are saved. As Scripture says, "Anyone who believes in him will never be put to shame." For there is no difference between Jew and Gentile—the same Lord is Lord of all and richly blesses all who call on him, for, "Everyone who calls on the name of the Lord will be saved"' (Romans 10:9-13).* However, this woman had already asked Jesus into her heart, so we simply reassured her and her loved ones of the promises of Scripture and what awaits us after death. We prayed, anointed her with oil, and comforted her and her family.

After performing the service for her near-death mother, we returned to her living room and began to fellowship. At this time the woman's anger returned and she stated that we had no idea how she was feeling. To which I replied, "You are correct Miss, we can't know how you are feeling, but we do have some level of understanding." "No sir, I don't think you do" she replied. To which I stated, "Miss, not many months ago, I buried a son." The room suddenly grew quiet and all eyes and ears turned to me. Then I said, "And Debbie buried her mother this morning." At this point, the angry woman began to cry with thanksgiving. She asked why would we come? I said we came because you called your church and you asked for help. Your church is here to meet your needs and to comfort you to the depth of our ability. The woman's anger was now gone, and thankfulness overwhelmed her. It is not always easy to love your neighbor, but we are God's ambassadors and the holders of His honor. He wants our obedience and faithfulness more than anything else. *"Therefore, as we have opportunity, let us do good to all people, especially to those who belong to the family of believers" (Galatians 6:10).*

God is the source of all things. Anything valuable inside you and me is there because God placed it there. We can add to those valuable things every moment of every day if we are willing to walk with Him. What we have to give to others is absolutely dependent on this truth. Because as Truth #2 declares, *"You Cannot Give Away What You Do Not Have."*

FATHER, I WANT MY LIFE TO BE SUCCESSFUL IN

Your eyes, to be a person after Your heart and to let Your love flow through me to those I meet. As I focus on becoming all You've created me to be, I know You will take care of all the other details.

8

TRUTH #3

YOU CANNOT MAKE SOMEONE ACCEPT
WHAT THEY ARE UNWILLING TO RECEIVE

Of all the promises and truths outlined in this book, Truth #3, *"You Cannot Make Someone Accept What They Are Unwilling To Receive"* may be the most difficult and challenging of all. It is totally necessary to include this truth because most people live in a results-oriented frame of mind. The thought of planting seeds and leaving the results to God is something most of us reject like the plague. Still, if we are unwilling to walk in obedience without the evidence of the fruit of our labor, we may end up pushing people away instead of attracting them closer to us. *"For we are to God the pleasing aroma of Christ among those who are being saved and those who are perishing"* (2 Corinthians 2:15).

To live out Truth #3 requires spiritual maturity, patience, longsuffering, and an unoffendable heart. If we are going to love our neighbor well, this truth must be on full display at all times in our lives. When we grow in our faith to a place where we can finally temper our desires of selfishness and begin to appreciate that each person will come to a place of understanding on their own time and in their own way, not because of our words, we will demonstrate great love.

A MUSCLE WE CAN EXERCISE

The world we live in today is offended at just about anything. The interesting thing about taking offense is that it's a choice. That's right, we choose to be offended. In the process of learning to live out Truth #3, we may become offended on many occasions ourselves. Learning to overcome the temptation to be offended will produce a crop of righteousness, joy, and peace beyond measure. However, achieving the distinction of "unoffendable" takes daily practice. *"And herein do I exercise myself, to have always a conscience void of offence toward God, and toward men" (Acts 24:16 KJV).* Like a muscle that we can exercise, the unoffendable heart is something that can grow stronger and stronger.

One of the great joys of our Christian walk is the day when we can genuinely say, "I am unoffendable." When a person can finally proclaim this statement, they know that God will help them fortify this declaration by continuing to bring more people into their lives that will allow them to grow stronger in their desire to remain unoffendable. God will do this because you are now ready to receive more from Him.

Let me explain how this works. Once you pick up the cup of the "unoffendable heart" (metaphorically speaking) and declare that you are unoffendable, you know that you will have to set the cup back down again. This happens because someone or something will cause offense in your life. Because you have demonstrated that you are ready for more of God in your Christian walk, God will grow you to be more like Him. Soon, you can pick up the cup of the "unoffendable heart" once again. You remain aware that at some point you will have to set it back down once again. The delightful thing about this exercise is that each time you pick up the cup, you get to hold it longer and longer. Conversely, you know that each time you set it back down, the cup remains out of your hands for a shorter and shorter time. What a great joy it is knowing that God will help us become more obedient so that we can offer ourselves freely without worry of rejection and truly love our neighbor as ourselves.

Before we get too far ahead of ourselves, let's recognize that being unoffendable is a two-part progression. First, we don't *take* offense, remembering it's a choice. Second, we don't *cause* offense. I have had numerous men tell me that this is impossible. They say there is no way to pre-determine how people will receive our words. I remind them that if our words are cutting and invasive, if we *Raca'* them, then we will cause offense with almost every person. However, just like the practice and exercise that we take part in to not *take* offense, we must put that same determination into practice to not *cause* offense. If our words are full of life and love and encouragement, the likelihood of us causing offense will be significantly reduced. *"Gracious words are a honeycomb, sweet to the soul and healing to the bones" (Proverbs 16:24).* Now, there may be times when loving our neighbor requires us to use words that would challenge a brother or sister in Christ, maybe causing offense. In those moments, I would suggest you rely on the Holy Spirit to direct you for guidance.

ARE WE THROWING OURSELVES AT PEOPLE?

We have all encountered a person, or two or three, who seem to poke their nose in places they don't belong. In all fairness, we have all probably done this on different occasions. When we begin to look at Truth #3, *"You Cannot Make Someone Accept What They Are Unwilling To Receive,"* discipline is crucial. We must take great care in our approach to who, what, when, why, and how we insert ourselves. We should never throw ourselves at people. Now, most people will gladly listen to you if you are sharing information about a fabulous restaurant and the great meal you had eaten, and most people will be eager to hear about the awesome movie you watched. Some might even want to hear where to go to get a fantastic deal on an item. I would even say that most people would certainly listen to you if you were sharing how nice and kind and warm and friendly, they are. There are, however, some people who shy away from compliments.

What would happen if you were sharing correction? Or you had information that would require a person to make huge changes in their life? Or if you were asked to be an accountability partner to someone? What if you knew with great certainty what a person needed to do to possibly remove the trials in their life? None of these instances would grant us a rightful stance to force anyone to receive the information or help we want to offer them. If delivered wrongly, it can look like we are throwing ourselves at a person who does not want to receive what we have to offer. This can bring problems to both parties. To love our neighbor, and to do it well, the discipline of discernment is necessary. *"But seek first his kingdom and his righteousness, and all these things will be given to you as well" (Matthew 6:33).* You would never walk into someone's home without first being invited in. In the same way, the best thing to do is to stand on the edge so you can be seen but wait until you are invited into their circumstances. Then you know they want to hear your contribution. As my mentor always reminds me, we are to give to those who ask.

REPEATED BEHAVIORS

Many of us know right from wrong but cannot break free from our pattern of sin. Even with constant reminders from our brothers and sisters in Christ, many continue to stumble.

"For I know that good itself does not dwell in me, that is, in my sinful nature. For I have the desire to do what is good, but I cannot carry it out. For I do not do the good I want to do, but the evil I do not want to do—this I keep on doing" (Romans 7:18-19).

I have been guiding, mentoring, and discipling Mark for many years. He is an avid church attendee and has a desire to walk deeper into his faith. Like many men, Mark seems to be caught in his past and often falls back into the familiar and comfortable ways he once lived. Every time Mark would take a step forward, a short time later he would inevitably take two steps backward. The world, for some, is just too appealing and they seem to never escape. Mark and I have had many conversations about how to move forward and what those decisions might look like for him, his girlfriend, and his son. One night, Mark asked me to pick him up, along with his family, and take them to a local restaurant so we could have a family discussion. Mark and his girlfriend stated that they wanted to live life the way God would want them to; the way the Bible outlined.

The first thing I shared was the importance of marriage, and the family structure. I was not insistent, nor was I forceful, but I was firm. Our conversation continued to outline the deeper meaning of marriage and what steps Mark and his girlfriend might consider beginning moving in the direction of Biblical marriage. It was then that both Mark and his girlfriend stated that this was going to be far more difficult than they had anticipated. They both shared concerns for their lack of faith and their unwillingness to change from the patterns of the world, including abstaining from sex before marriage. It was then that I shared that human beings are habitual, people of patterns or routines. Mark asked me what that meant? I stated to him and his girlfriend a simple fact, "Every day that you demonstrate the life that you are currently living to your son, is another day that your son will be sure to repeat it. I can most certainly guarantee this. If you want more for your son, you will have to show him what that looks like." Mark and his girlfriend heard my words that night, knowing they were laced with truth and love. However, time would indicate they weren't yet ready to fight off the comfort of their familiar patterns.

Sometimes loving our neighbor can be extremely difficult, especially when we cannot make someone accept what they are unwilling to receive.

STUNNED TO SILENCE

Sometimes we encounter people whose lives are so out of control, lost and adrift in the darkness of the world, they can't begin to see their way out. They are so far from God they will grab at anything, try anything, or say anything to make themselves feel like they are doing something positive. When God places a person with these kinds of circumstances in your life, you can be sure He is wanting you to reach out and invade the person's space. He wants us to reflect His light and help open the eyes of the blind. *"The night is nearly over; the day is almost here. So let us put aside the deeds of darkness and put on the armor of light. Let us behave decently, as in the daytime, not in carousing and drunkenness, not in sexual immorality and debauchery, not in dissension and jealousy. Rather, clothe yourselves with the Lord Jesus Christ, and do not think about how to gratify the desires of the flesh"* *(Romans 13:12-14).*

George was the last man we were waiting for on Friday. His name was on the list to be part of our cabin for the weekend retreat. Nobody knew George, but we waited intently for him anyway. George did not arrive until Saturday afternoon and I did not meet him until late Saturday evening. While we were talking as a group in the cabin, that evening, George suddenly opened up. He began to share how grateful he was to be on the retreat even though he had just met us. He felt like he could feel God and trusted us. That is when the bombshells started exploding. George stated that he was divorced and that he had three children. He also stated that he was self-employed and earned a hefty wage. George told us that he had a $1,000 a week cocaine habit and all his money went to feeding his addiction. Each week he would enter the most depraved neighborhoods to get his next fix. Sometimes he would even have his children with him while buying drugs. In fact, George disclosed the reason he failed to arrive on Friday was because he needed a fix. His mother had purchased his ticket to come to the retreat because she felt like it might do him some good. Most of the men in the cabin had never heard such things and were stunned to silence.

At this point, we began to minister to George as a group because he needed to feel God's love. After a series of inquisitive questions and some sincere listening, George said he wanted to give his life back to the Lord forever. George exclaimed that he knew the Lord because he grew up in the church and his father was a pastor. We talked a little while longer and then prayed that God would heal George and restore his life. George left the retreat that weekend with his phone full of the numbers of his new friends. Unfortunately, nobody ever heard from him again. Not for the lack of trying. Sometimes, we must use whatever means necessary to share the love of Christ with the person in front of us, but that does not mean that the person will accept what he, or she, is unwilling to receive.

HOW MANY?

Over the years, there have been many men who have asked me to disciple them. I have learned that not every "ask" is an all-in genuine desire to learn and grow in the Lord. The world is a difficult place to navigate for many people. A great number of men reached out for help because their lives had become overwhelming. We spend a few weeks together and then their interests grow cold. A few weeks pass by and they reach out again. Try as they might, they just cannot get into the habit of placing God first. If I want to love them in the way that God loves me, I have to freely offer myself to them, time and time again. It seems very few people have explored the idea of discipleship, as it is not popular in our culture. Because of this, we tend to remember vividly those who have participated in the merry-go-round of insincere discipleship.

Once, I was asked how many men do you, disciple? I responded, "If I begin to entertain answering the question, it is no longer about obedience to God, but about serving my ego." Many men have come and gone, and I welcome them whenever they show up. At this, the person persisted, "Why do you continue to let them come back time and time again?"

I replied, "Because they are not mine, they are God's. He has entrusted me to walk with them, whenever and wherever they show up."

Truth #3, *"You Cannot Make Someone Accept What They Are Unwilling To Receive"* is not easy to live out. If I want to love my neighbor, I must be willing to accept it. ***"Dear children, let us not love with words or speech but with actions and in truth" (1 John 3:18).***

9

TRUTH #4

YOU CANNOT TAKE SOMEONE TO A PLACE
YOU HAVE NEVER BEEN

I f you have ever raised children, you will certainly understand what I am about to say. We are not always present *in* the moment. People can recognize when we are "with" them or when our minds are off in the distance. The latter is something that nearly every parent has demonstrated to their children at varying times.

Imagine you are attempting to repair something in your home, or are at the grocery store with limited time, or are talking on the phone and your child approaches you with a question, wanting your attention. In many of these moments, we greet the child with a pacifying response because our minds are preoccupied. The child emphatically knows you are attempting to pacify them. If these pacifying moments occur with any consistency, they become our go-to response whenever we are engaged in something and another person contends for our attention.

Just like our children can spot our agitated and/or pacifying responses a million miles away, so can a person who is desiring our guidance or empathy because they are in a dire circumstance and need attention. If we are not careful, this pattern of behavior will show a lack of empathy for the person's trials and tribulations. One can tell whether this has been exposed in themselves by the responses they offer to those in need. You may say things like "I know how you feel" or "You'll be fine" or "Heaven has another angel." The point I am attempting to make here is that applying Truth #4 *"You Cannot Take Someone To A Place You Have Never Been"* is the difference between loving someone or adding to their discomfort.

When we don't have the same personal experience as the person we are attempting to comfort, we should use fewer words and more actions. ***"So may the words of my mouth, my meditation-thoughts, and every movement of my heart be always pure and pleasing, acceptable before your eyes, my only Redeemer, my Protector-God" (Psalm 19:14 TPT).*** We don't have to pretend that we know anything about how they feel or their current circumstances to love them. If we attempt to be anything other than authentic in these circumstances, those who are receiving this bogus affection will smell our stench in an instant. It will only get worse from there.

GOD WASTES NOTHING

God allows a crisis to get our attention, and then He uses the crisis to develop our character. Every person will experience trials and tribulations of various kinds and at different times. I have heard it said that we are either about to enter a crisis, in the middle of a crisis, or leaving a crisis. Knowing this, will we allow God to mold us into something we weren't before the trial? *"Consider it pure joy, my brothers and sisters, whenever you face trials of many kinds, because you know that the testing of your faith produces perseverance. Let perseverance finish its work so that you may be mature and complete, not lacking anything" (James 1:2-4).*

For most people, the thought of finding joy during a trial is anything but pleasant. In my life, I have seen many trials. Some of them occurred as a young boy when I did not have a relationship with the Lord. I spent years trying to understand why these things happened. As I grew stronger in the knowledge of the Lord and my faith began to mature, I learned to take the verse from James as literal. I can clearly see today how God uses all our trials for His glory as He brings those across our path who are experiencing difficult moments that we have also endured. I can only speak for myself, but I have seen God use me to help others who have had uniquely similar experiences. When I begin to speak to these individuals, it is truly astounding how they hang on my every word. I have come to realize that there is relief in knowing that someone else has had similar experiences. Some might call this street cred, but I know that God wastes nothing.

A FENCED-IN BACKYARD

I can't count the number of men I have counseled either during a divorce or after their divorce was final. There are also many couples I have had the pleasure of helping through some challenging seasons of their marriages. What is more, most of these problems were more complicated because children were involved. It's no accident these people find their way into my life. If you know anything about divorce, you know that couples in the throes of it usually have a very difficult time maintaining their self-control. As a result, the children suffer even more than the issues of the divorce would cause.

This is where God uses my childhood to help people recognize mistakes they might otherwise make with their children. I consider myself a bit of an expert on this subject because both of my parents entered into marriage three times. Each time, they repeated the same mistakes as before and even managed to add to the number with each new marriage. My brothers and I suffered as a result of having been cast in five different families. Because God has healed my wounds, I can help men, as well as couples, find their way through this challenge.

As I mentioned, reducing the number of mistakes that one makes in the course of divorce is extremely important. Mistakes will be made. The focus should never be on achieving perfection. The most important thing to remember is that one has to address the mistake(s) quickly. *"Fathers, do not embitter your children, or they will become discouraged" (Colossians 3:21).* If a child is wounded by actions or words and the mistake is not corrected when recognized, hopefully sooner rather than later, a scar will form. Once formed, it may be carried for life.

Another thing I impart to people in these types of situations is to remember that the child never wants to hear either parent talk negatively about the other parent. Usually, people entering divorce are so angry and hurt they blame the other parent for all the ills of the marriage. When this occurs, it's not very long before the child is being told that mom or dad is a bad person. Another thing that is often overlooked is the level of worry, fear, and anxiety that a parent projects in front of their child. Most people don't realize that the child will rise to the level of anxiety that they see in their parents.

The last thing that I share with every person that I counsel in these areas is a metaphor that involves every child. Children want a fenced-in backyard, in fact, they crave a fenced-in backyard. Once their fenced-in backyard no longer exists they begin to long for one. What is the fenced-in backyard? For children, this represents safety, serenity, peace, and hope. You would think that these realities are common knowledge, but it has been my experience, they are not.

THE FATHER WOUND

"Sing to God, sing in praise of his name, extol him who rides on the clouds; rejoice before him—his name is the Lord. A father to the fatherless, a defender of widows, is God in his holy dwelling. God sets the lonely in families, he leads out the prisoners with singing; but the rebellious live in a sun-scorched land" (Psalm 68:4-6). Father wounds are inevitable. Some people are walking this earth with a papercut because their fathers knew how to address the wounds that were inflicted. But others are walking around with torn flesh and exposed organs because they have been slashed to pieces with samurai swords. Their fathers said they loved them but did not know how to demonstrate their love. Their fathers simply followed the example they saw. A father's rejection of his child is probably the most dominant and destructive force this world has ever known, as it can lead to generational curses that leave untold devastation. Healing from a father wound is never swift. Let me say that again, healing from a father wound is NEVER swift! Sometimes the wounds follow us relentlessly.

My grandmother had just died. After making some of the

funeral arrangements, several members of the family assembled at her house to reflect on her life. As I was preparing to provide her eulogy, I began to ask my family for their thoughts. I wanted to make sure that everyone's voice was heard. My uncle began to recall his memories. All of a sudden, he stood up out of the chair. He walked to the front window, looked out, and said, "He's coming this time. He promised!" There was no thought behind this action, just muscle memory. He was four years old when my grandfather left him, my aunts, my mother, and my grandmother. A father wound so deep it cut my uncle to the core. Nearly 65 years had expired, and he still bleeds profusely. I was astonished at what I had just witnessed.

Many have a wrong view of God the Father because they have a skewed view of their biological father. Healing begins when we realize that Father God loves us deeply. I am thankful that God has healed me of my father wound. My father's choice was the same as every other father that has ever lived; break the curse or leave it for the next generation to deal with. Unfortunately, I could not experience forgiveness *with* my father as I was forced to take that journey alone because Truth #2 reminds us, he did not have it to give away. It took me many years to learn to truly forgive my father, but I can now walk with others who have yet to find healing and show them the way.

Truth #4, *"You Cannot Take Someone To A Place You Have Never Been"* is like a key that unlocks doors for others to enter. God entrusts us to lead people to the places we have been.

AND LIFE GOT BETTER

I remember the day my wife called me and shared the news that she had cancer. Like most people, my thoughts were racing with all sorts of predictions, not all of them were good. Over the next few months, many questions flooded my mind. I never prayed harder or longer, and I never saw the glory of God so vividly. As difficult as that season was for my wife, in a very odd way, God made things better and my wife was healed. *"Then Jesus said, 'Did I not tell you that if you believe, you will see the glory of God?'" (John 11:40).*

As my wife was nearing her five-year mark, we would get yet another scare. Oddly enough, on Christmas Day 2011, the doctor in my family (my brother-in-law Jake) said that something was wrong, and I needed to make an appointment. Three short weeks later, I was on the operating table to remove a large cancerous tumor. During recovery, I would see the glory of God in ever greater measures and life got better. Nearing my five-year mark, a scheduled screening test indicated that cancer had returned. I was off to surgery once again. God showed up in ways that He had not shown up before and life got better. It was then, that I asked Him,

"God, every time cancer shows up, You swoop in and life gets better. But how many times will cancer show up? And how many times will You continue to make life better?"

Since then, I have learned not to ask those types of questions. God does not owe us any answers. What I do know is this, I now have new places to take people. I can minister to a greater number of people and cancer has allowed me to make hundreds of hospital visits, home visits and to speak to people who are facing a similar diagnosis. God gets the glory because my wife and I are healed, and I get to proclaim His goodness. I can love my neighbor because I have walked in some very specific shoes.

THE LOSS OF A SON

The worst of all the trials I could ever imagine is one that never leaves me. Every day I am cruelly reminded of the loss of my son. Since that awful day, I have experienced affliction, a pain, a gnawing at my soul that words cannot describe. It's a constant lament, but I have never asked God the question of "why." I know that God understands what I am experiencing and the pain that I feel. I know that He will never leave me. *"The Lord is close to the brokenhearted and saves those who are crushed in spirit. The righteous person may have many troubles, but the Lord delivers him from them all; he protects all his bones, not one of them will be broken" (Psalm 34:18-20).*

Since the death of my son, now 14 months later, God has brought 20 men across my path who have lost children of their own (take note that God continues to increase the number of encounters). By the grace of God, my lament leaves me during the times I am allowed to minister to these people, and joy emerges within me knowing that I can take these people to a place that I have been. Yes, it's a place that they fear, a place that no one enters willingly, a place that no parent should ever have to stomach.

Some of these people have lost more than one child. Some have even lost two in the same instance. Most human beings can easily get caught up in their pain, trials, and tribulations believing that no one else has ever experienced the level of grief or pain that they know. The loss of a child is an affliction that even the evilest person would dare not wish upon anyone. However, after encountering several parents with multiple losses, I quickly realized that theirs is a pain much deeper than I can understand, nor that I want. Through this perspective, we learn to empathize and love our neighbor well.

I HAVE BEEN THERE

I have lived through all of these experiences shared in this chapter, some longer than others, some I still stare at daily. Actually, each of the topics spoken of in this chapter could be titles of books and dissected more closely. God has graced me with healing and blessed me with understanding. Now I have the privilege of being one of His chosen vessels to help people with similar instances. Those who choose to listen and apply the information can benefit during the storms of life. I don't share the information because I read it in a book, or because I heard it from a friend. I can take people to these places because I have been there. Your experiences are probably different from mine. My hope is that as you love your neighbor, you take each person to the places you have been. It's in those moments that each of us encounters God. *"All this is for your benefit, so that the grace that is reaching more and more people may cause thanksgiving to overflow to the glory of God"* *(2 Corinthians 4:15).*

FATHER, I AM HOLDING ON TO YOU AND NEVER LETTING GO. THOUGH THE WINDS OF DISTRESS AND

TRIAL BLOW, YOU ARE MY ANCHOR. I WILL WORSHIP
YOU AND TRUST YOU DESPITE THE CIRCUMSTANCES.
USE THIS TIME TO HONE ME AND DRAW ME CLOSER
TO YOU. USE ME TO MINISTER TO OTHERS WHO HAVE
LOST THEIR WAY AND CANNOT SEE THROUGH THEIR
BROKENNESS.

TRUTH #5

TIME IS A NECESSARY COMPONENT FOR UNDERSTANDING

W hy do we insist on believing that we can change people? Why don't we understand that we can only demonstrate, guide, or plant seeds but that real change is for God to accomplish through the individual? Why do we convince ourselves that we would be satisfied with the change that we believe we have encouraged in a person? Forcing a perceived outcome is never change, and it will never be long lasting because the individual did not bring it forth. Love never forces, it demonstrates grace and mercy and brings *awareness*.

A person is helpless to change anything without *awareness* and the Power of the Holy Spirit. Once awareness intrigues the mind, understanding can begin to grow. Once understanding begins to develop, a person may begin to apply what they have learned. Once the information is applied consistently and becomes rooted, it can remain a part of the person. True change has now occurred, and a new behavior has developed. All of this requires *time*, and of course, willingness. Thus, Truth #5, *"Time Is A Necessary Component For Understanding"* is an essential ingredient to loving our neighbor.

In fact, the same increase of understanding that invites change in our neighbor is the same invitation in the increase of understanding we must welcome in ourselves. Sanctification is a lifelong process, not a fleeting event. As we all grow in the likeness of our risen Savior, let us not forget that love is patient, always hopes always perseveres. While we learn to *walk the talk*, our demonstration will inspire others to do the same. *"I won't hesitate to continually remind you of these truths, even though you are aware of them and are well established in the present measure of truth you have already embraced. And as long as I live I will continue to awaken you with this reminder" (2 Peter 1:12-13 TPT).*

We all need constant reminding and course correction so the depth of truth and understanding God has for us can continue to grow and remain firmly rooted.

INVEST IN PEOPLE, NOT PROGRAMS

One of the reasons that discipleship has become less attractive in some churches is because it requires willing parties on both sides, someone to give and someone to receive, and takes great sums of energy and time. In some cases, the development of any single person can barely be measured. When we read in the Old Testament book of *Exodus 3:6, "Then he said, 'I am the God of your father, the God of Abraham, the God of Isaac, and the God of Jacob,'"* we find a very distinctive clue to genuine discipleship. We may never know if what we are offering, as one discipling others, will have any results until the person being discipled produces a disciple of their own. This is a measure of true discipleship and it does not produce tangible numbers in the short term. Most discipleship programs include a series of processes, procedures, books, and schedules. These types of programs allow for variables or metrics to measure their successes. Once a person completes grid "A," we are ready to move them to grid "B." Once a person completes books I and II, they are ready for books III and IV. Or are they? Did every person find understanding? Are they truly ready to graduate to the next level?

Maybe for some the answer is "yes," but for most, the answer is "no."

I was once sent a video on discipleship that was more like a marketing scheme. This video claimed if one man were to disciple 1000 men a year, it would take 15,000 years to cover the globe. However, if one man were to disciple one man for a year, and that process was to be duplicated repeatedly, the globe would be covered in under 50 years. Sounds perfect, doesn't it? Once you begin to examine the elements that this marketing scheme neglects to take into account, you quickly understand why it is flawed. It assumes every person starts in the same place, every person retains information at the same rate, every person has the same life experience, and every person needs the same equipping. It neglects the simple fact that life happens, and changes occur regularly. There will be many interruptions that will cause delays such as deaths, illnesses, job loss, etc. The last and most important thing that this marketing scheme fails to address is the relationship. Without a relationship, you have nothing! Personal interaction, trust, connectedness is different from one person to the next, meaning that not every person has a personality that relates to all. There are people that I will never be able to disciple simply because our personalities don't click.

I believe we must refrain from anything that says, "If you complete (this), you will look like (that)." A wise man once told me "Invest in people, not programs." All of this is to say that Truth #5, *Time Is A Necessary Component For Understanding*" also has a very distinctive feature attached to it. Time! The window of "time" is different for every person if we desire to understand. Thus, Truth #5 is another important element to loving our neighbor well.

FIRST IN THE LINE OF 1000

"We are therefore Christ's ambassadors, as though God were making his appeal through us. We implore you on Christ's behalf: Be reconciled to God" (2 Corinthians 5:20). How many times have you found yourself in a conversation with someone and suddenly you realize that they are not saved, they have never given their life to Christ? You share the gospel and wait, but nothing happens? What about the family member, the friend, or the loved one that you desperately want to be saved but you know they are not? Do you stand in front of them and think to yourself, "I am not leaving until they give their life to Christ?" Or are you willing to find the joy of knowing that you have been entrusted by God to share His love and light with the world?

It's difficult for most of us to embrace the fact that our journey to understanding is just as necessary and important as the person we are spending time with. Continually growing in the knowledge of the Lord Jesus Christ removes our desire to create an outcome or change the person to whom we might be ministering. What if you are the first person in the line of 1000 to plant the seed of God's love?

Are you willing to allow God to have His way? Are you willing to walk in obedience? Are you willing to give what you have when the opportunity presents itself? Truth #5, *"Time Is A Necessary Component For Understanding"* applies both to the giver and the receiver.

NOT IN A MILLION YEARS

Sometimes God will bring understanding in the most astonishing ways and through the most unlikely events and through the connection of people who are unaware of what is happening until His splendor is revealed. It's through these types of occurrences when God will uncover a single thread in the fabric of our lives, and we will see unmistakably that He has woven us together for His glory. When this understanding comes, we often begin to realize that the more we know, the less we know and that God is God, and we are not. *"My goal is that they may be encouraged in heart and united in love, so that they may have the full riches of complete understanding, in order that they may know the mystery of God, namely, Christ, in whom are hidden all the treasures of wisdom and knowledge" (Colossians 2:2-3).*

Our church held a men's retreat and although I did not attend, God made a way for me to be an integral part of the outcome. At this retreat, a man died of a heart attack. He collapsed near his cabin. The men who found him gave him CPR for over an hour to no avail. As you would expect, every man present was deeply affected. The following week, I was asked to "emcee" our Tuesday night Men's Group because our leader was out of town for work. Before the night began, I approached Al and told him that I was going to share the Gospel with the group. I asked Al if he would say a salvation prayer for anyone who might want to leave the night with this gift. Only one man accepted the invitation that night, his name was Bill. Some months later, Bill would send a prayer request to the church because his mom was battling cancer. Bill was unaware that each prayer was answered personally. Randomly, I was given this request. I called Bill and after some small talk, I realized we had previously met. Bill shared about his mother's cancer and then he asked me, "Where is God in all this?" I reminded Bill of the night at the men's group, some months earlier, when he gave his life to Christ. I asked Bill, "Where was Al sitting that night?" He said, "Al was right next to me, why?" I replied, "I asked Al before arriving that night if he would usher the salvation prayer to anyone who may be ready to give their lives to Christ. You asked me where was God in all of this? He is all around you. In a sea of more than 100 men, how did Al end up right next to you that night?"

A few months later, Bill would approach me at church wanting prayer for his mother. He asked if I would come to his mother's home the next day and spend some time with her. I agreed. Sadly, a few hours later Bill called to let me know that his mother had passed away but asked if I would still come as planned. When I arrived, I saw a large gathering of people walking back and forth between houses and children running around playing. Bill informed me that all these people were family members and one house belonged to his mother and stepfather, and the other house belonged to his father and stepmother. They were neighbors and the best of friends, in fact, his stepmother was his mother's primary caregiver during her battle with cancer.

When I saw the children able to approach any of the people without reluctance or apprehension, I asked Bill how was this possible. I was amazed that the innocence of the children had been preserved and they could approach any of the adults, knowing that love was awaiting them. Bill informed me that his mother loved Jesus Christ and her faith was the catalyst for everything that I was witnessing. I could see that Bill was wondering why I would ask such a question. I told him that I had been searching for this *oneness* in my family since I was 9 years old, it never materialized. We prayed, laughed, and cried together.

When I got into my car to head home, I called my brother and told him what I had witnessed, what we had been missing our whole lives. I was so thankful to finally see that blended families can function together and make unity work, and Bill was a recipient. When I entered the funeral home for Bill's mother, he and I shared some light conversation. However, I was still reeling from what his family was able to accomplish. It was then that he told me that his mother and stepmother were writing a book, "Not In A Million Years," the story of how two women, in the most unlikely of circumstances, would find friendship and bridge their families in love. How did God take the death of one man, back at the retreat, and turn it into all these events for Bill and me? Both of us found enlightenment even though we did not seek it. Sometimes understanding comes at a time you least expect. *"He has made everything beautiful in its time. He has also set eternity in the human heart; yet no one can fathom what God has done from beginning to end" (Ecclesiastes 3:11).*

I WILL COUNSEL YOU

I remember a time many years ago when I was new to my faith and I lacked understanding but did not know it. One Sunday, I was walking through the halls of the church I was attending, and a man approached me who said that he was a representative for a group of men who were going to begin to disciple other men. He asked if I would like to join the group and be a part of their mission. Without thinking, I answered, "Yes, of course." As soon as I walked away, I began to entertain multiple questions in my mind. These questions persisted throughout the following week. Why did he approach me? What would this look like? Do I have the time necessary to participate? Am I equipped to disciple another man?

Before the next Sunday came, I had convinced myself that I was in no position to say yes. Therefore, I sent a message to the man who had approached me with some lame excuse why I could not participate. Almost immediately, I began to wrestle with this choice because in my gut I knew that this was something I was supposed to do. *"I will instruct you and teach you in the way you should go; I will counsel you with my loving eye on you" (Psalm 32:8).*

Fast forward a few years. I found myself spending a lot of time with many men helping and guiding them in their struggles, their current circumstances, and explaining how to deepen their faith. Some years later I would meet my mentor, Loren. Through our time together, he would bring an awareness to me that I was unable to see before meeting him. He helped me discover that I had been discipling men but did not truly know it, nor did I understand it. Through his mentorship, my skills were honed and continue to be sharpened today. In fact, not long ago, Loren asked if I would like to be ordained by him and the Master's Christian Ministries. He said that this ordination was not the beginning of a journey but an acknowledgment of the calling on a man's life.

I agreed to the ordination and we made plans to schedule the event. In preparation for the day, Loren asked me to spend some time with a couple of individuals who would also be presenting at the ceremony with him. When he shared the names of these men, my mind began to race with awe, excitement, and gratefulness to God. One of the men Loren named was the same man who had approached me all those years ago with the question, "Would you like to join our group as we begin to disciple men." I thought, only God could do such things. After much time, I now had a greater understanding. If there were any remaining doubts as to what I was supposed to do with my life, God had just erased them all. Now I have another added, and necessary, detail to love my neighbor well.

Let us never forget Truth #5, *"Time Is A Necessary Component For Understanding."*

11

TRUTH #6

GRACE + TRUTH + TIME = CHANGE

W hy do we resist change? Change is the only constant in life. Every day of our lives we are gently forced to make adjustments. As we navigate our day and make these adjustments, we are almost unaware they occur. *"Therefore we do not lose heart. Though outwardly we are wasting away, yet inwardly we are being renewed day by day" (2 Corinthians 4:16).*

The alarm clock did not go off on time and now our morning schedule has just become shorter than we would like. The road we are traveling on is under construction and we have to find an alternate route. Traffic is backed up because of an accident and we are forced to find another avenue to travel. The store where we choose to do our shopping does not have the product we want, and we have to find a different store. Our car breaks down and for the next week, we have to make other arrangements to get to work. A meeting at our child's school is brought to our attention at the last minute and we have to juggle our schedule to attend the meeting. Our boss asks for a report by the end of the day that we thought was not due until the end of the week, so we are required to shuffle our day to meet the demands. The restaurant where we have decided to eat dinner is over-crowded, so we have to find another place to eat. The piece of equipment we want to utilize at the gym is not available, so our workout program is forced to change. The list seems to go on and on, but it serves to awaken our minds to the endless adjustments we entertain daily.

These changes continue to occur without warning and with very little resistance because life continues to happen, and we must find a way to complete our day. Which of us would stop our day completely, not moving on to the next task, because of these minor variations? The answer is, none of us. However, when we are forced to take control of the changes in our lives, including those we desperately desire, we resist change like the plague. Have you noticed this? If we seem to have no trouble making the adjustments of daily life, why do we struggle when we have to be in control of the change in our lives? Why are we so obsessed and overly crit-ical of the changes we want to see in others? Why do we have such limited patience while waiting for the changes of those around us?

Truth #6, *"Grace + Truth + Time = Change,"* explains simply and accurately that the equation for change is different for every person. If we are going to love our neighbor well, perhaps we should learn to apply this truth.

UNENDING LOVE

If we want to see a change in others, we must also recognize the need for change in ourselves. Here we can turn our focus back to Truth #2, *"You Cannot Give Away What You Do Not Have."* God uses people and circumstances to stir changes within us, so we can help others make changes within themselves. In doing so, each of us discovers that the full measure of Christ is within us as God's Word reminds us of in 2 Peter. What is more, the equation in Truth #6 helps us to see that we slowly *clothe* ourselves with the richness of Christ, constantly supplementing our faith towards unconditional love. Except, who are the people that God would choose to walk this journey of change with us? Will we see them coming? How beautiful it is when they are revealed.

"Everything we could ever need for life and godliness has already been deposited in us by his divine power. For all this was lavished upon us through the rich experience of knowing him who has called us by name and invited us to come to him through a glorious manifestation of his goodness. As a result of this, he has given you magnificent promises that are beyond all price, so that through the power of these tremendous

promises you can experience partnership with the divine nature, by which you have escaped the corrupt desires that are of the world. So devote yourselves to lavishly supplementing your faith with goodness, and to goodness add understanding, and to understanding add the strength of self-control, and to self-control add patient endurance, and to patient endurance add godliness, and to godliness add mercy toward your brothers and sisters, and to mercy toward others add unending love. Since these virtues are already planted deep within, and you possess them in abundant supply, they will keep you from being inactive or fruitless in your pursuit of knowing Jesus Christ more intimately" (2 Peter 1:3-8 TPT).

I did not initially see Seth as a person who would both give me grace and help me walk in grace. It wasn't until the second chance encounter that we would even speak to each other. God told Seth to lay his hand on my shoulder and invite me on a journey of a deeper faith. Seth was obedient. Less than two weeks after meeting Seth, he asked me to take a trip to Buffalo, New York with him for a revival. To ensure that I would not say "no," Seth insisted that all expenses were on him, I simply needed to pack a bag.

Have you ever spent time with a person that was so full of the Holy Spirit and Truth of God that their fruit was overflowing? Insert a picture of Seth. His faith was inspiring, his words were powerful, his grace was Spirit-led, and his love was from the Father. How do we know when a person's heart is *all-in*? If we consider that the heart is the distributor of life (blood) to the body, you can easily tell when someone's heart is in something because there is life in what they are doing. It is evident in their words and their actions. If you ever meet Seth, you will quickly gain this understanding, he's *all-in*!

In Buffalo, we participated in a foot-washing ceremony for all the people in the Bed & Breakfast where we were staying. That included the owners, hired hands, and residents. We visited several churches in the surrounding communities sharing in prayers and the laying on of hands for the healing of the sick. We visited a working farm that housed men who were recovering from addictions. We would sit and minister to them and experience church on site. We phoned a man the locals suggested would provide wisdom and insight into the things of God. After spending an afternoon with this man and sharing a meal with him, we felt like we had experienced the Holy Spirit. Our last night in Buffalo was spent preaching in the lobby of the B & B to all the people staying there. Seth continues to challenge me to walk in grace.

Seth and I have taken many more trips together. Each time, grace abounds, and it is never without truth. Seth remains consistent to this day as a man walking in the Spirit. He has never shown me anger, frustration, condemnation, or contempt. His love is unending. He challenges me with the grace of God every time I am with him. Seth also continues to lavish me with generosity. Rarely will he allow me to pay for a meal or a trip. He has shared with me that God told him to lay his hand on my shoulder, he has yet to hear God say stop. So, Seth will continue to do so until God tells him otherwise.

Where did Seth come from? I did not search him out. God's grace brought us together. God says His grace is enough! It is His grace that brings forth change. The last time Seth and I were together, he said he knows for certain the things he shares with me are being shared with hundreds and maybe thousands of others and God is glorified.

Truth #6, *"Grace + Truth + Time = Change!"*

CHRIST'S AMBASSADOR

There are times when God will entrust to you the responsibility of demonstrating His grace to a person you did not know was coming your way. You undoubtedly don't know who the recipient will be, and you may not be certain of what the person's response will be. All you know is that God has asked you to be His ambassador and share His love wherever you go. *"We are therefore Christ's ambassadors, as though God were making his appeal through us. We implore you on Christ's behalf: Be reconciled to God. God made him who had no sin to be sin for us, so that in him we might become the righteousness of God" (2 Corinthians 5:20-21).*

Robert was a man, among many other men, who would share a cabin at the start of a weekend retreat with total strangers. When the weekend was complete, the men would be strangers no more. Robert knew his faith was deficient and he needed an infusion of truth and hope. To be blunt, his faith was wavering, his marriage was rocky, his household was crumbling, and his life was empty. For six weeks prior to the retreat, Robert had prayed every day that God would send someone to bring accountability to him. This was the weekend he hoped would bring renewed strength and confidence. That was the sole reason he came. Robert listened intently when each person in the group would speak. He and I spent a lot of time together that weekend. Robert asked many questions about faith, Scripture, and his purpose.

When the weekend drew near its close, Robert approached me and asked, "Could we spend more time together? What can we do to make this possible? I prayed that God would send someone, and I am convinced He sent you." I assured Robert that his desires were possible, and we began to meet weekly. Robert and I have met every week since that weekend and his life is vastly different. He has a purpose, his marriage is strong, his house is in order, and his faith is growing.

Robert would tell you that God is constantly calling us and asking us to walk with Him. He would tell you that God sends people who would act on His behalf and provide the stability we need in times of trouble. These people will offer His grace, they will share His Truth, they will give His time. Soon enough, we will clearly see change! All we have to do is respond with a "yes" and have the courage to walk. Truth #6, *"Grace + Truth + Time = Change!"*

IN THE WORLD AND OF THE WORLD

For some of us, God will create a circumstance that will span untold years and will bring glory unto Him because there is no other way to explain the outcome. *"If the world hates you, keep in mind that it hated me first. If you belonged to the world, it would love you as its own. As it is, you do not belong to the world, but I have chosen you out of the world. That is why the world hates you" (John 15:18-19).*

It was 1990, I had no idea who God was, and I surely did not know His Son, Jesus Christ. One day I walked into the fabrication shop where I was employed. Most people did not like entering this place because Scott, the manager, was the crudest, rudest, and nastiest person I have ever met in my life. That day, I walked into the fabrication shop to find Rob pinned in the corner by Scott. Scott was calling Rob all sorts of foul things. He was pushing, punching, and belittling Rob! Why? Why would someone do such a thing? As Rob walked into the fab shop that day, Scott was gazing at a porno magazine and wanted Rob to look as well. Rob refused! Why? Rob was a Christian! But the more Rob refused, the angrier Scott became and the more he physically accosted Rob.

As I watched this unfold in front of me, I began to cheer Scott on. Yes, you heard me correctly. It pains me to share this story. I was both *in* the world and *of* the world at that time. ***"You adulterous people, don't you know that friendship with the world means enmity against God? Therefore, anyone who chooses to be a friend of the world becomes an enemy of God" (James 4:4).*** I was not a Christian, but I was a human being. Still, I did nothing to stop this from happening. What occurred thereafter, astounded me. This godly man, Rob, watched me watch him be physically and verbally assaulted for not wanting to dishonor his God. He watched me cheer this event on and still Rob decided that I was worth loving, in spite of everything that had happened. Rob had every reason to never speak to me, never forgive me, even to hate me, but that day Rob decided to make me his friend.

That day, I watched someone stand up for something bigger than himself. I was not sure what that something was, all I knew was this, Rob was willing to be persecuted for it. Rob became the first person to speak truth into my life. Rob shared many things with me and helped me begin a journey, the best journey I have ever known! Where did Rob come from? I did not search him out. God brought us together. God's grace is enough! It is this grace that brings forth change. ***"As God's co-workers we urge you not to receive God's grace in vain" (2 Corinthians 6:1).***

Over the years, Rob has been one of the most important spiritual mentors in my faith walk. He and I still speak every six months or so and try to get together at least once a year. In the Fall of 2015, I was speaking to Rob on the phone. Rob began to recall the great transformation that had taken place and how much God had changed my life. It was then that I reminded Rob of that awful day some 25 years earlier. That awful day, and at the same time that glorious day! Rob said that he indeed remembered. I informed Rob that he owned a piece of my Christian walk. The day he demonstrated the grace of God, my life was changed, because Rob was willing to plant a seed.

We both cried and praised our Lord and Savior. Rob then asked me what else was new in my life? I informed him that cancer had returned once again, and I was getting ready for more surgery and chemo. This time the doctors were telling me that after this surgery, I will no longer have a voice. They were certain that my vocal cords would need to be severed to remove the cancer. When I awoke from surgery, I began to wonder, had God delivered me from cancer, for the second time? Do I have the ability to speak? These thoughts were quickly removed when I opened my eyes and the first person I saw was Rob. We both cried and we praised our Lord and Savior! Truth #6, *"Grace + Truth + Time = Change!"*

SERVING SELF?

God is always aware of our heart and the things, apart from Him, that would become important to us. Each of us has times when our hearts are selfish, and we serve our flesh. Often these moments of blindness occur without our knowing or realizing it. This is why we must continually practice turning our attention to the One who Authors our faith.

We had just commissioned our latest group of Stephen Ministers, and the Midweek Service had ended. Paul approached the pastor with a dilemma and needed some help. The pastor called for me and introduced me to Paul. Paul had a very unusual request. He stated that his father had died, days earlier, and that the funeral home viewing was set for the next day. Paul was concerned that there would be very few people in attendance as his father was nearly 100 when he died and most of his father's friends were already dead. To keep his family from suffering any humiliation, Paul asked if I would gather some of the people from the church and assemble them at the service. I tried my best to honor his request but wasn't able to, and I was the sole person to attend.

On my way to the funeral home, I convinced myself that this was my opportunity to share wisdom and insight. I was going to do this. I was going to do that. I was going to share. I, I..I... you get the picture. Little did I know that God had other plans. At the funeral home, I sat close enough to the family to be available if they needed me but far enough away not to be in their personal space. It was an extremely long day. Time passed slowly and I began to talk to God. "God, I have never been more uncomfortable in my life. I am sitting in a funeral home at the request of a man that I have known for all of 10 minutes. Besides Paul and his mother, not a single person has spoken to me all day." I heard nothing from God in return. When the time of visitation had drawn to a close, I started to get excited with the idea that this most uncomfortable day was over. Paul thanked me for all I had done, but he had one more request. Paul asked, "Would you be a pallbearer tomorrow for my father?" I thought, could this day get any more uncomfortable? How did I get myself into this situation? I placed Paul's needs above mine and answered, "Sure I will."

That night on the way home and the next day en route to the service, I had many conversations with God. I realized that I had let my ego get the best of me and was sure this was going to be another extremely uncomfortable day. Walking into the church and taking my place with the other pallbearers, I was stared at by nearly everyone in the room. I am sure they were wondering who I was and why I was among them. While listening to the eulogies of the dead man's children, God brought clarity to me. Each child, two sons, and a daughter shared differently. One son spoke of the great dad the deceased had been. The other son spoke of his father's many great accomplishments. The daughter spoke longer than both sons combined. She thanked all the people who had given their time to her father in the last 12 years of his life as he fought cancer and needed constant support. I found myself grieving, openly weeping, for a man that I had never met. I had just experienced love in a way that I had never experienced before. All the uncomfortableness had been worth it. That's when God said to me, "You let pride get in the way My son. Then you gave the control back to Me and something amazing happened. Aren't you glad?"

"Beloved ones, God has called us to live a life of freedom in the Holy Spirit. But don't view this wonderful freedom as an opportunity to set up a base of operations in the natural realm. Freedom means that we become so completely free of self-indulgence that we become servants of one another, expressing love in all we do. For love completes the laws of God. All of the law can be summarized in one grand statement: 'Demonstrate love to your neighbor, even as you care for and love yourself'" (Galatians 5:13-14 TPT).

Truth #6, *"Grace + Truth + Time = Change!"*

12

FINAL WORDS OF WISDOM

I believe the 4 Promises and 6 Truths are a gift that God bestowed upon me. Each catchphrase on its own is not unique. In fact, most of us have probably utilized many of them in our conversations and our relationships. It's not until you bind them together in different combinations that they become unique. This is the revelation that I received from God as I have witnessed all of the catchphrases as beneficial throughout my ministry in the pursuit of loving my neighbor as myself. God gave them to me, and I now give them to you.

My prayer is that you would find the 4 Promises and 6 Truths valuable enough to apply them to your relationships and together we could experience more of the love that God has for us. The 4 Promises and 6 Truths are not meant to entangle our minds and hearts into some mechanical interface with the people we encounter. They are a tool that can help us understand that loving our neighbor requires us to free ourselves of ourselves and let God have His way. So let us, instead, learn to "wrap" or entangle ourselves with the living God so the people He brings into our path can experience His great love.

We should never forget that our presence is much more valuable than anything we can ever say or do. We are vessels of God's love, instruments of God's peace, and reflectors of His light. Not always are words necessary. It is reassuring to know that any combination of the promises and truths that I have shared in this book can be utilized when words are necessary to comfort and love others.

Maybe you have experienced the lack of love in the world? I sure know I have. My belief for this definite emptiness in our culture and our relationships is simple; we continue to push God aside. When we live according to our own understanding and not lean on His, things tend to go wrong for us. If we love our neighbor, why do we compare ourselves with others? If we love our neighbor, why do we criticize others for their beliefs? If we love our neighbor, why do we get angry when someone attains material wealth that we don't have? If we love our neighbor, why do we call other people unpleasant names? If we love our neighbor, why do we unfriend people from social media?

Love comes from God. Love is a gift that we can have more of if we are willing to receive more from the Source that is love. That would require us to walk more closely with God. Sadly, most of us believe that we are good enough on our own and we can muster all the love that other people deserve from the broken cisterns we call "self."

The 4 Promises and 6 Truths have helped me to relinquish control back to God. If we are going to love our neighbor well, it will require us to swim upstream, go against the current culture, and rely on God, not ourselves. *"So you must remain in life-union with me, for I remain in life-union with you. For as a branch severed from the vine will not bear fruit, so your life will be fruitless unless you live your life intimately joined to mine" (John 15:4-5 TPT).* We must resist the idea that we are good enough without God. As a mentor of mine once told me, "Don't play God but take Him with you wherever you go!"

WITHOUT HIM, WE CAN'T BUT
WITHOUT US, HE WON'T

What would it take for us to allow the root of love to be planted deep within us? How can we begin to see roots so connected to the source that we would lose ourselves? We must continue to trust that God can do immeasurably more than we can ever imagine. We must grow in the understanding that apart from Him we can do nothing, but "with God all things are possible." We must continue to grow and understand that He can multiply our offering when we are rooted in His love. *"And I pray that he would unveil within you the unlimited riches of his glory and favor until supernatural strength floods your innermost being with his divine might and explosive power. Then, by constantly using your faith, the life of Christ will be released deep inside you, and the resting place of his love will become the very source and root of your life" (Ephesians 3:16-17 TPT).*

In the year 2000, my wife and I purchased a brand-new conversion van. Our sons were young, it seemed like the right vehicle for our needs. My wife was not a fan at first. However, over the years, she grew to genuinely enjoy the van.

She drove our sons all over town, to practices, games, and friends. When that season of life was over, when our sons no longer needed to be driven around, the van became impractical, so we parked it in the driveway. After six months, I grew tired of looking at the van and told my oldest son that he and I were going to clean it up and sell it.

The next morning, I received an email from a prayer group, stating that a family was experiencing hard times and in desperate need of a vehicle. After speaking with my wife, we agreed that God was asking us to give our van to this family. Later that day, my son and I began cleaning the van to make it presentable. When we had finished, my son said, "Wow, Dad, the van really looks nice!" I agreed but paused for a minute. My son asked what was wrong? I told my son that I was sure that God wanted us to give this van away. At the same time, I felt like we were giving away a damaged vehicle, and that bothered me. The rear seat was inoperable, it had quit working almost six years earlier. It was electric and converted from a seat to a bed. The boys pressed the buttons so many times, over the years, that the motors seized, leaving the seat stuck in between, not quite a seat and not quite a bed.

My son suggested that maybe we could push the seat back into position. I lifted the skirting from under the seat to show my son all the motors that no longer worked. I told him that we could never overcome the mechanical advantage of the motors. The seat was frozen in this position. At that moment, my son decided to push the button that controlled the seat. To our astonishment, God made it move into the seating position. We both sat there for a few minutes trying to comprehend the miracle. Remember, for nearly six years the seat would not move. We had newfound excitement and delivered the van to the waiting family. On the drive home, my son asked, "Dad, how did all this happen?" I told him that God wants our obedience, He wants our hearts, and He wants us to love our neighbor. My son said, "Dad, I still don't understand how this all happened." To which I replied, "Son, without Him, we can't but without us, He won't."

YOU GET GOOD AT WHAT YOU PRACTICE

The journey of 1,000 miles begins with the first step. A marathon is completed by consistently placing one foot in front of the other. Every endeavor we face requires that we be persistent so that we can become better. Musicians must spend 10,000 hours to master their instrument. Most anything we attempt to accomplish requires practice. We get good at what we practice. *"Whatever you have learned or received or heard from me, or seen in me—put it into practice. And the God of peace will be with you" (Philippians 4:9).*

My friend Dave once said to me that he loves everyone, probably more than they love him. I asked him how he could be so sure? Dave, a retired police officer, said that if a gunman were to enter the premises, he would protect the people and run at the person with the gun while everyone else ran for cover. I told Dave that what he had described was both honorable and courageous, but that it did not necessarily mean that he loved more than someone else. His continuous training as a police officer had allowed him to overcome two of the three distinct responses of human nature. In those types of circumstances, we either fight, flight or freeze. Dave's 30 years of strict training structured him to fight out of a duty to protect, not necessarily out of love. I then asked Dave what would happen if he were to give God 30 years of strict training in his faith? What a powerful weapon he could become for God's Kingdom.

In the same way that we practice our job every day so that we can become more efficient and more valuable to the company, we must also give God the same steadfastness. In fact, God deserves far more than we give to our careers. I have found that *practicing* the 4 Promises and 6 Truths has helped me to love my neighbor *well*. You may also find that they can benefit you in your longing to love your neighbor *well*. After all, you get good at what you practice!

WHY DO YOU CALL ME LORD?

The Bible mentions the word Savior very few times, but the word Lord occurs thousands of times. Where do you think God places the emphasis? You can't come to Jesus as Savior and make His Lordship an optional package to consider later! We must surrender to Him thoroughly, completely, and swiftly. *"Why do you call me, 'Lord, Lord,' and do not do what I say?" (Luke 6:46).* Loving our neighbor is not supposed to be a "choice" we make, but a command He proclaims. I have witnessed many people follow the command of the Lord. Sometimes what He asks is simple and sometimes it is grand.

Many years ago, I was talking to my brother on my cell phone while watching my son play soccer. He was hearing the news about my wife and her diagnosis of cancer. What I did not know was that people were listening to my conversation. After hanging up, Dawn approached me. We had said hello to each other about a half-dozen times before because our children were on the same team. Dawn said to me, "I could not help but overhear your conversation. Sorry for eavesdropping, but God just told me to throw your wife a fundraiser." I said, "Excuse me? What did you say?" Dawn said, "God just told me to throw your wife a fundraiser." I was absolutely flabbergasted. After a brief moment of confusion, I continued, "You are going to what? Who are you? Why? How?" Dawn said that it may take her a while to organize everything but rest assured when the event was planned and scheduled, she would get back in touch with me.

A few months later, Dawn had everything ready. My entire family attended the event. As we entered, we were overwhelmed with the number of people who would come to support my wife. Dawn had organized a spaghetti dinner and arranged for multiple businesses to secure a silent auction. In total, Dawn's obedience managed to serve over 750 dinners and raise more than $15,000 for my wife's medical bills. I remember thinking, "God, I don't even know this woman. How in the world could this be happening?" That's when God decided to exhibit His grandeur in a way that only He can.

The evening was nearly over when a man in a wheelchair approached me. He wanted to know if this event was in honor of my wife. He wanted to know if my father's name was Ken. He wanted to know if my father had grown up in East Detroit. I responded, "Yes, yes, and yes." Then, the man in the wheelchair introduced himself as John G. He acted as if I somehow knew him or should at least remember him. I was puzzled because I did not know him at all. So, I apologized to him. That is when he told me that he and my parents lived on the same street from the age of three until the age of twenty. In fact, he lived right next door to my mother and directly across the street from my father all those years. I explained that my parents, aunts, uncles, and most of the rest of my family had left the event already. I wondered how they did not run into each other. John said that people change over time and he had not always been in a wheelchair. I was saddened that John had missed all of them. I asked,

"John, what brought you here?" John said, "My daughter threw this event for your wife." I sat down and cried. When you think you have seen the best that God has to offer, be prepared to be stunned over and over again!

I can't begin to find words that could accurately describe the events that led to that evening. God told a woman to throw a fundraiser for a complete stranger. I witnessed her obedience and God changed our lives forever. Only He can do such things. If Dawn had not known God as Lord, I would never be able to share this experience of God's extravagant love with you.

FATHER, I PRAY THAT WE WOULD BE ROOTED AND GROUNDED IN YOUR LOVE. MAY WE EXPERIENCE YOUR AMAZING GRACE EACH DAY. HELP US TO KNOW YOU AS LORD SO THAT YOUR GRACE WOULD EMPOWER US TO STAND WITH CONFIDENCE AND MAKE THE WORLD A BETTER PLACE. SEARCH US FATHER AND SEE IF THERE IS ANY OFFENSIVE WAY IN US. MAY WE BE YOURS-WHOLLY.

SEARCH ME, GOD

I ask you now to think about applying the information from this book to your life. The 4 Promises and 6 Truths have become a wonderful help to my faith journey. God has clearly shown me that this is valuable by all the wonderful blessings and fruit He has provided to my life. When you are asked to explain, "How do you love your neighbor?" maybe you can pass along the wisdom of this book.

If you allow God to have control of your life, I promise that He will take you places that you never thought you would go, allow you to meet people that you never thought you would meet, and do things that you never dreamt were possible. This book has provided a glimpse into my life, the life that God has blessed me with, the life I never thought possible. Ask God to search your heart and help you begin a journey into His Kingdom. What do you have to lose... but your life? *"Search me, God, and know my heart; test me and know my anxious thoughts. See if there is any offensive way in me, and lead me in the way everlasting" (Psalm 139:23-24).*

NOTES

Foreword
Philippians 1:9-11

Chapter 1- Make It Simple
Luke 10:25-37
Daniel 5:11
1 John 1:1
Psalm 128:1, 73:26
2 Corinthians 9:6
Philippians 2:17

Chapter 2- Promise #1 - I Will Never Judge You
1 John 4:7-8
Hebrews 4:12
1 Corinthians 13:13
Galatians 5:22-23
Colossians 3:12
Mark 10:27

Chapter 3- Promise #2 - I Will Never Be Your "Yes" Man
Matthew 5:22
Proverbs 12:18, 21:23, 13:20
Colossians 4:6
Ephesians 4:15
James 3:10
1 John 2:17

Chapter 4- Promise #3 - I Will Always Point You To Jesus
Matthew 16:15-16, 28:19-20
J. I. Packer, Knowing God (Downers Grove: Inter Varsity
Press, 1973) 21
2 Corinthians 4:5
Matthew 7:21
1 Corinthians 12:13
Ephesians 3:20

Chapter 5- Promise #4 - I Will Always Have Open Arms Ready To Receive You
Luke 15:20
Romans 3:10-12
Ephesians 5:1
Philippians 2:3-5
Galatians 5:16-17
1 Peter 1:22

Chapter 6- Truth #1 - Once You Learn A New "Truth", You Cannot Unlearn It

James 1:22
2 Timothy 2:2
Matthew 7:13-14
Eugene Peterson, Working The Angles (Grand Rapids: Wm. B. Eerdmans, 1987) 162
James 1:5
William Law, Power Of The Spirit (Dallas: Gideon House Books, 2017) 112-113
Author Unknown, Quote
Romans 8:28
Matthew 6:34
1 Corinthians 13:12

Chapter 7- Truth #2 - You Cannot Give Away What You Do Not Have

2 Peter 3:18
Matthew 5:13-16
Romans 15:13
2 Corinthians 1:3-4
Matthew 5:46
Romans 10:9-13
Galatians 6:10

Chapter 8- Truth #3 - You Cannot Make Someone Accept What They Are Unwilling To Receive

2 Corinthians 2:15
Acts 24:16
Proverbs 16:24
Matthew 6:33
Romans 7:18-19, 13:12-14
1 John 3:18

Chapter 9- Truth #4 - You Cannot Take Someone To A Place You Have Never Been

Psalm 19:14

James 1:2-4

Colossians 3:21

Psalm 68:4-6

John 11:40

Psalm 34:18-20

2 Corinthians 4:15

Chapter 10- Truth #5 - Time Is A Necessary Component For Understanding

2 Peter 1:12-13

Exodus 3:6

2 Corinthians 5:20

Colossians 2:2-3

Ecclesiastes 3:11

Psalm 32:8

Chapter 11- Truth #6 - Grace + Truth + Time = Change

2 Corinthians 4:16

2 Peter 1:3-8

2 Corinthians 5:20-21

John 15:18-19

James 4:4

2 Corinthians 6:1

Galatians 5:13-14

Chapter 12- Final Words Of Wisdom

John 15:4-5

Ephesians 3:16-17

Philippians 4:9

Luke 6:46

Psalm 139:23-24

ABOUT THE AUTHOR

 Jeff is a Chaplain, teacher, mentor, pastoral care provider and an author. He lives with his wife Laura in Shelby Township, Michigan, and they have been married for 30 years. He is a father of three sons, two adults and one deceased. He has served in various organizations over the years in the community in which he lives. Jeff is involved in discipling men in several churches, and currently has a home-based fellowship in Shelby Township where he serves as a pastor.

Jeff's passions include reading, writing, teaching, mentoring, counseling, and discipling men. He is a life-long learner and shares this knowledge with the dozens he counsels and serves. He is also founder/president of GRAM Ministry. His ministry, of almost two decades, has primarily been in small groups and one-on-one encounters.

Many long-established spiritual leaders have poured into Jeff over the years. He believes this spiritual capital God has poured into him should be invested into the lives of others. Jeff spends his days encouraging men to receive the grace of our Father in Heaven and to trust Jesus, His Son, as their life source and purpose.

Made in the USA
Columbia, SC
12 December 2021

51146730R00115